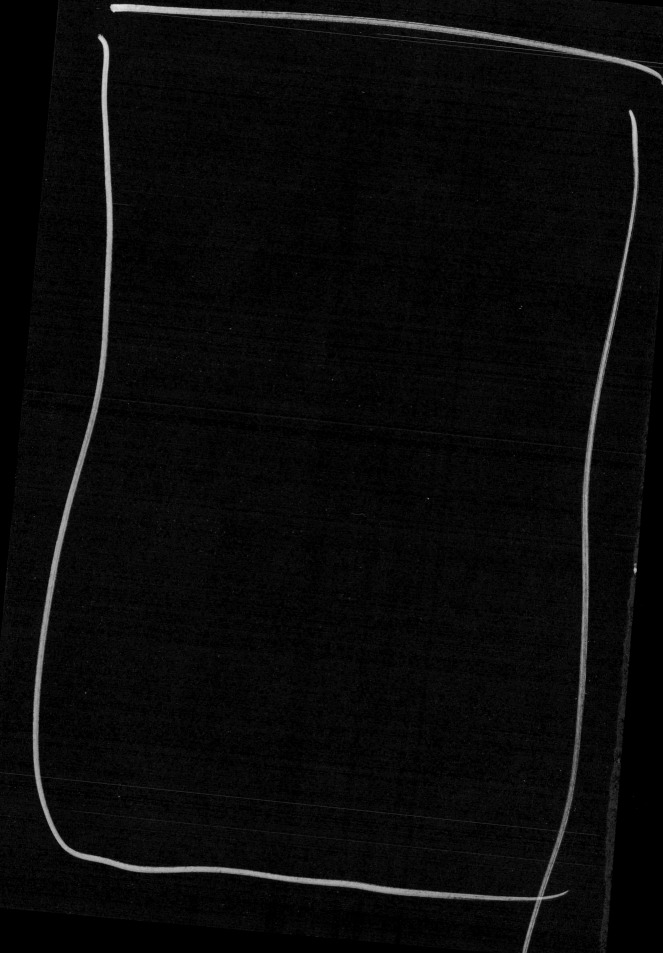

RISUS SARDONICUS

RISUS ✻ SARDONICUS

For Jonathan Oakes
with warmest best wishes
for a great future
Warren
5/28/10
Boulder

Warren Martin Hern

2009

Published in 2009 by
Alpenglo Graphics • www.alpenglographics.com
All text and photographs copyright © Warren Martin Hern 2008
1130 Alpine Street,
Boulder, Colorado 80304

Design & production: Pauline Christensen, Longmont, Colorado

Photographs of woven handpainted Shipibo cloth for cover and half-title:
  Ken Sanville, Louisville, Colorado

Library of Congress Control Number: 2007900890

ISBN 0-9792205-0-5

CONTENTS

This book is dedicated to
the memory of the Ibo baby
who I saw dying of tetanus in the
hospital at Abakaleke, Nigeria,
in August 1961.

PREFACE

EVEN THOUGH THIS BOOK contains only my writing and my photographs, and it is my sole eccentric idea, it could not happen without the expert assistance of many people to whom I am extremely grateful. First of these is Polly Christensen, who is officially listed as the designer of the book. But Polly is also a dear friend, a thoughtful editor, an extraordinarily creative and skilled person, and, perhaps most of all, someone who consistently and tranquilly says, "Okay, fine, what about this?" instead of "WHAT? YOU CAN'T DO THAT!"

Also, I must thank my photographer friend and image magician Ken Sanville, who helped me prepare and assemble many of my photographs, and the very smart laboratory people at PhotoCraft who helped me with others.

The Shipibo people have taken me into their homes, lives, and hearts since 1964. I cannot thank them enough for that. They have had much to do with shaping my life.

There are many people in my life who inspired the writings in this book, and I am grateful to all of them whether the inspiration was pleasant or unpleasant or otherwise.

—WARREN MARTIN HERN

IRK

Even though
        I
               find
                      it

irksome,

           now and then
           I
        have
   to

           work some.

PROSTATE POWER

To have power in America

You must have a prostate

Bigger than your brain.

1

SMALLPOX

In 1964, in between my third and fourth years of medical school, I spent six months working in the Peruvian Amazon. During the first few months, I worked as a physician-in-training at the *Hospital Amazonico "Albert Schweitzer,"* which was founded in the early '6os by a German physician, Theodor Binder. Binder had been a protégé of Schweitzer, and he built his small hospital and compound on the banks of Yarinacocha, an ox-bow lake linked to the Ucayali River about 10-kilometers downstream from Pucallpa. Pucallpa, a frontier river town of about 30,000 when I arrived there that year, was the major town and port city in that part of the Amazon, and it still is. Up and down the Ucayali for hundreds of kilometers and radiating out from the river were countless Indian villages and small Mestizo towns.

After working at Binder's 28-bed hospital for about three months, seeing thirty to forty patients an afternoon in the outpatient clinic, performing surgery every morning with an Italian-American doctor who had come down from New York to fill in for Dr. Binder while he was away, and generally running the hospital, I arranged to go out to one of the Shipibo Indian villages to do some anthropological research. I wanted to learn about the concepts of health and illness held by the indigenous people in that region, and the Shipibo village of Paococha was my starting point. I collaborated with a young Peace Corps volunteer, Frank Billman, who was doing community development work in the village and helping with the hospital-sponsored agricultural cooperative.

For two months, I lived in the village and conducted my research, which included a house-to-house survey of health problems, a census, and long evening sessions sitting with the *muriah* (native healer) as he worked. My teacher, a diminutive old man named Benito, cooked and mixed his *oni* (also known to outsiders as *aya huasca*—"dead man's vine") during the day, then drank the hallucinogenic potion during his healing session. I listened to his songs and conversation with the *isinibo* (sick ones) who came to see him. Benito and I referred each other patients; we developed a kind of collegial relationship. He was better at psychotherapy than I was, especially in Shipibo, but I had more antibiotics and worm medicine. And I could set broken bones.

Eventually, my participation in the *jonibwensuate* (healing session) included my ingestion of the *oni*, which did, indeed, have a powerful hallucinogenic effect—much to my alarmed surprise. With Benito and another friend, I took notes concerning the Shipibo mythology, cosmology, and concepts of illness.

Just as things were really getting interesting and I didn't want to leave, it was time to return to Colorado and my last year of medical school. I reluctantly headed out on a barge I caught upriver from Pao. But by this time, the people

 2

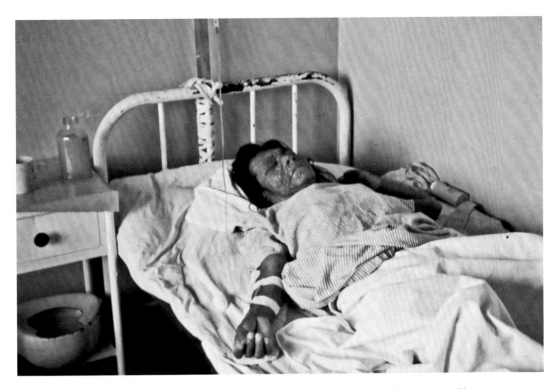

had decided they wanted me to train three young men chosen from the village to be *sanitarios*—first-aid corpsmen, so to speak. I agreed to meet them at the hospital and teach them a few things before returning home. One was my friend and age-mate, German, the village chief at that point; the second was Helio, who became my best friend in my whole life and with whom I worked closely until his tragic death in 1996. The third was Virgilio, a bright young schoolteacher.

My plan was to leave the Amazon right away so I could spend several weeks traveling in the Andes before going on home.

When I arrived at the hospital, a new set of facts presented themselves. There was a smallpox epidemic in the Peruvian Amazon. Not recognizing the disease, doctors had hospitalized several patients, and others contracted the scourge. I talked with a missionary doctor friend of mine, Ralph Eichenberger, who had given me inspiration and invaluable advice, and he told me of whole villages being wiped out by smallpox throughout the region. He and his fellow missionaries were working hard to save the people they were serving.

Through Ralph and the pilots at the Summer Institute of Linguistics, a missionary bible-translation base on Yarinacocha, I arranged for one of the pilots who was heading out for Iquitos in a week or so to land on the Ucayali River by Pao while he was en route and deliver to us some live smallpox vaccine that had to be kept refrigerated.

Meanwhile, my Shipibo buddies showed up at the hospital. Abbreviating the *sanitario* training, I taught them how to help me do the smallpox vaccination procedures. One man would write down the names of those coming for the vaccination, one would wipe the skin clean with acetone, one would place a droplet of vaccine on the cleaned skin, and I would perform the skin-puncture vaccination.

A few days later, straining to meet the schedule of the float plane landing on the river, we set off in a large, open dugout canoe for Pao. The river was low in the dry season, and it was hard to keep from hitting logs or running aground. The *vueltas* (meandering loops) of the Ucayali were immense and time-consuming. We hit a log and broke a propeller. We stopped and cooked *ipo* (a primitive armored sucker fish) on the beach. We were devoured by mosquitoes. At about 4 A.M. we stopped at Sharamashu, a few dozen kilometers upstream from Pao, so that a couple of guys could run back into the bush to tell the people in that village to come to Pao in three days for the vaccination. As we were sitting on the riverbank waiting for them to return, listening to the river flow by with its sounds of jumping fish, night herons, and cayman (a kind of alligator) hunting for fish, and watching the brilliant Amazon night sky, one

of the Shipibo men said, *"Mire, doctor, una satélita!"* There we were, hundreds of kilometers from any major city in the middle of the Peruvian Amazon frontier, and a satellite passed over us. It was an astounding moment.

As we approached Pao in the starlight, we could hear a plaintive, melancholy wail coming across the water. *"El hijito de viejo Lucho se murió,"* said one of my companions. Old Luis Ramirez had his house right on the riverbank at the port. His infant son had just died. The women were mourning. Lucho was weeping as he fashioned a casket from part of an old canoe in the pre-dawn light. We paid our respects and passed on down the path to the village.

After a little breakfast, Helio and German set off with some others for the villages downstream. Colonia Roaboya was the Shipibo village and the original settlement. Roaboya was a Mestizo town of about 500 that had a state school and elected officials. Our plan was to vaccinate the people from Pao and Sharamashu on the day the plane arrived with the vaccine, then ship down to Roaboya for the vaccinations of the people in those two settlements.

While there was cooperation, there was also tension. The Mestizo (mixed) people of the Peruvian Amazon at that time viewed the Shipibo as subhumans and treated them accordingly. For the Mestizos, the Shipibo, whom they called the *"Chama"* (a term much like "nigger"), were objects of scorn, derision, exploitation, and violent abuse. In turn, the Shipibo deeply distrusted the Mestizos in general, and they hated some of the most abusive and exploitative Mestizos. The two groups lived side-by-side and needed each other, but the animosity was profound.

The float plane set down on the river on the appointed day. It was flown by Bob Hettema, a Korean War Air Force veteran pilot who was both incredibly skilled and extremely funny. It was a remarkable moment.

We immediately set up our primitive outdoor clinic and vaccinated all the people from Paococha and the upriver villages by the end of the afternoon. The next day, we loaded the vaccine and other supplies into the dugout and set off downstream for Roaboya. We were met by the village authorities and the local schoolteacher, who offered to let us use the one-room elementary school for the vaccination program.

Walking through the line was a young man, Augusto Flores, who had a very large leg. I examined him in the corner and found that he had an enormous cancer on his upper leg that extended from the knee to halfway to his hip. It was about a foot in diameter and hard as a rock. I sent him up the river to the hospital by way of the mail boat. Later, after I took some x-rays of this, I had him sent to the cancer hospital in Lima, where they took off his leg at the hip. He had a chondrosarcoma (cancer of the cartilage), a highly malignant form of cancer. Five years later, Augusto gave me a ride on his boat from Pao to Contamana on my way back home. He was getting fat from drinking the beer he was supposed to be selling. I saw him standing by the road with his crutch one day several years ago when I was riding a rickety *colectivo* from Yarinacocha to Pucallpa.

After we finished vaccinating the Shipibo from Colonia Roaboya and the Mestizo citizens of Roaboya, the *teniente gobernador* (mayor, sort of, of the village) invited me and my Shipibo friends to have lunch at the local *tienda* (shop), the closest thing to a restaurant in town. I immediately accepted the offer. We all sat down in the schoolhouse to visit while the meal was being prepared.

In time, the *teniente gobernador* said we could walk over to the *tienda*. We were accompanied by the *agente municipal* (police chief, sort of), and the *profesor* of the school. The *autoridades* showed me up the steps into the *tienda* and into a small dining room just big enough to contain one table set with four places. My Shipibo buddies were nowhere to be seen. "Where are my *compañeros?*" I asked. "Oh, they're eating out in back with the help," the *teniente* replied. "No, they eat with me," I said.

The *autoridades* froze in disbelief and embarrassed silence. They looked at each other for a few seconds, then the *teniente* said, "We'll call them to come here."

A few minutes, later, my three Shipibo friends came filing into the room and I motioned them to be seated. The four of us sat down to a very nice meal of beans, rice, fried bananas, and stewed chicken. The *autoridades* stood and watched us as we ate, trying to make conversation.

The Shipibo have never forgotten this incident. It is one of the reasons I am a *shipibaopanebaque* (adopted son of the Shipibo).

There were no cases of smallpox on our stretch of the river.

RISUS SARDONICUS

black woman

    doctor

        walking brisklydowntheaisle

    between

        the

        two

        rows

        of

        beds

nodding and smiling
            into
                the

        isolation

           room

   clouds of steam rolling out

a woman looked up sadly from a cradle to the

                  eyes of the physician

  sharp

   short

    cry

     stretchingviolentlymouthtwistingtoa

    tortured sarcastic smilefrown

          then

         pucker

    tremblejerk

the mother bent over the child speaking softly in

             Ibo

   and looked again at the younger

    woman

we must try anyway said the doctor.

SWAMP SOLDIER

I can't breathe or swallow
I cough all the time, and
I hurt down here.

These are the only people
that ever wanted me
and I don't want to leave them.

She's ugly, sir, but she's
all I want.

I found her in the swamp, sir.
She ain't much, but she's mine.

I love her, sir.

I don't need money,
I live in the swamp, sir.
We have a witch doctor.
I can go back to the swamp.

I don't hate other white men.
I just hate their ways.

CIGARETTE ROMANCE

Brush your burning butt

To mine.

A ROSE FOR TANYA

A lovely rose
        for a lovely woman

A passion flower
        for a passionate heart

A fragrance
        to match yours

A vivid color
        that betrays my feeling

A blossom
        that has opened
            in my heart

THE URGE TO VERB

—A postmodernist cybernetic lament

Have some herbed rice, she said
Who herbed the herbed rice?, I asked

The urge to verb is everywhere

Who herbed the herbed chicken?
How do chickens feel about
Being herbed? Moreover,

Who will herb the verbs
Or verb the herbs?

Is it botanical
Semantical
Semiotic
Hermeneutic
Emic
Etic, or
Emetic?
Ick.
Let me out of the attic
And pass the emesis basin, please.

How impactful.

The contextualization
Is impacting me impactfully.

The commodification is
Nonsensing me,
Distancing me
From reality,
But not as much as
Parents parenting,

Apparently.
Pasteurize the milk, please.
Don't let this past yer eyes.

The verbification of nouns corollaries
The complification of language; thus,

Thundershower activity instead of
Rain.

What happened to Fred?
He got to nouning verbs and was participled
To death.

Even though I am addicted to the
Verbification of nouns,
Will you interface with me
On the Net?

Hope those wholes in the Net are big enough
For freefall verbification
And small enough that
You don't fall thru.

Well FAX me down,
Beam me up.
I'll be faxed.

And I have the urge to merge with you.

Who owns pre-owned cars before they are
owned?

"Pre-boarding is available now," The
attendant says.
How do I preboard?
Where in space and time does that occur?,
Ask I.

How can you pre-board before you board
Unless you are bored with the ennui,
With boarding on time in real time?

When is a pre-born child not a child?
When it is only a thought
Or just an urge
To merge?

Being birthed
Is of no consequence.

Who is the birthor and who the birthee?

To birth or not to birth.
Is it worth the mirth?

I hope no one decides I am a pre-dead corpse
And tries to bury me.

Merging Traffic, the world says enigmatically.

The sign says "Yield,"
Not "Give Up."

BRAZILIAN GIRLS

Brazilian girls

    aren't giants

        mental,

           but they

        are very

    ornamental,

And they rouse in me

        an impulse that is

           simply elemental

OS ALAGADOS

THE PRINCIPAL CITY in which I served as a Peace Corps physician from 1966 to 1968 was Salvador, Bahia, on the northeast coast of Brazil about a thousand miles north of Rio de Janeiro. Salvador, a very African city in many ways, was the first colonial capitol of Brazil. In addition to its basic Brazilian vitality, it retains much of its rich African heritage in music, rhythyms, colors, food, art, language, and exuberance. But the poor people of Bahia express their love of life in spite, sometimes, of the most crushing poverty and misery imaginable.

In the lower part of the city, a peninsula juts out into the *Bahia de Todos Os Santos* (Bay of All Saints) and then curves back toward the city. In the crook of this peninsula lies a low area that is flooded at high tide. A large community of makeshift houses on sticks is built out over the tidal flat. The *bairro* (neighborhood) is called *Os Alagados* (the flooded areas), and it was notorious for its squalor and tragedy. One walks on rickety planks over the water, decaying garbage, trash, rotting fish, sewage, and flotsam brought by the tide. The city garbage trucks dump in the area, and the garbage becomes part of the unsanitary land fill. People make their living sifting through the garbage for food and items of value. It is not unusual to spot a dead baby in the litter heap.

An outstanding Peace Corps volunteer of that time, Elizabeth, lived with the people in the Alagados. The people loved her. So did I.

One day I walked with Elizabeth out some ways into the Alagados on the wobbly planks to visit a woman with twins who was so poor it was difficult for her to get enough food for her babies. She was alone with them. She wailed her misfortunes to us. The twins were hungry and they were sick. She was sick. Her arms were thin, little more than bones. Her face and eyes were sunken. The twins were dehydrated from diarrhea. There was no drinking water. There was no way to wash clothes.

Her situation was not unusual.

Elizabeth's role was to work with the community, such as it was, and the Maryknoll priests who were there to help, so that organizations could be formed to help people like the woman with twins.

Robert Kennedy came to visit the Alagados as a U.S. Senator. Elizabeth was his guide. She went back to Pennsylvania. Kennedy was assassinated.

The Alagados are still there. I don't know what happened to the woman and her twins.

PEOPLE

people
said the cab driver

are a pain
in the ass

MISERY

misery

      is when
      your girlfriend
      tells you
      she
      can't
      make love
      with you
      anymore

      because

      she has learned
      from her
women's liberation group

      that
      having sex
      with men
      is

      counterrevolutionary

COMPLICITY

I have resigned myself to
temporary
complicity with evil
in order
to accomplish certain
strategic things

for people

whose suffering is more important
than my need
to maintain
moral purity.

PIE

the apple pie was delicious

and so are you

PROGRESS

Progress

Isn't.

LIMITS

There is no limit
To human stupidity.

There is definitely a limit
To human intelligence.

UP THE UCAYALI

BY MY THIRD VISIT to my Shipibo Indian village in 1974, I had been a visitor enough times to have been accepted into the community. In fact, an old man named Pastor Ochavano, who had been chief of the village in his youth and with whose daughter's family I stayed during my research, had given me my Shipibo name, *Caibima* ("The traveler who comes from afar but who always returns here"). I had become part of the family.

Another person whose family became mine was my friend German Cairuna, who was my exact age mate (our birthdays were a few days apart). He had been chief of the village when I had first visited in 1964. His parents, Leoncio and Lasthenia (also known by her Shipibo name, *Inimuë*—"Sweet-smelling herb"), had adopted me informally as a son. When I was to travel, Inimue would give me a delicious lunch of *rira*: made of roasted *sungaro* (a kind of large patterned catfish) mixed with yucca, a starchy plant, water-turtle eggs, cilantro, and *aji* (a small hot pepper). This mixture was wrapped in fresh banana leaves and roasted.

As I was about to end my four weeks of field research, German brought me a large basket of water-turtle eggs, which were considered a delicacy and a highly prized source of concentrated protein. We boiled them for the trip.

Often I would travel up and down the river on barges or ships that were carrying freight on the Ucayali. This time German and his family needed to take produce to Pucallpa and visit relatives. About eight of us, including part of another family, crammed into a dugout canoe fitted with a 9-horsepower Briggs & Stratton air-cooled engine. The engine was ingeniously mounted on a swivel with a long propeller assembly fixed to the motor, and the result was a highly maneuverable craft in the rather dangerous waters of the upper Amazon. The shallow draft permitted us to cross near beaches and save time as well as to land on the beaches to camp and cook. The trip up the Ucayali took about two to three days depending on weather and conditions. We often traveled at night, with me holding a flashlight in the prow. Flying fish would crash flopping into the bottom of the canoe. The kids slept in their mothers' arms.

Sometimes it rained, and the days in the open boat were hot. I had an old army poncho for protection.

Our destination, Pucallpa, was a frontier river town of about 40,000 with a waterfront, dirt streets, innumerable outdoor markets, and tiny shops and bars busy with travelers and adventurers. There were few amenities of civilization. The "port" for small craft like ours consisted of a large mud flat of several square miles. It was the dry season and the river was receding, so there was no defined river bank. As we arrived, we beached the canoe as close as we could to

solid sand, but nothing was dry. I stepped onto the mud and sank up to the mid-calf or deeper with each step.

As I got out of the boat, shouldered my load, and prepared to hike the five or six kilometers to the center of town and a hot meal, one of my fellow passengers, a woman named Rosalia, spoke to me in Shipibo. *"Caibima. Huë. Bihuë."* ("Caibima, come here. Take this.") Then she took a necklace from around her neck and placed it around mine. The necklace was very simple, consisting of a string of small, dark-grey seeds from the "Jacob's tears" plant. She stepped back and looked at me. *"Joribihuë,"* she said ("Come back").

When I arrived at the Hotel Gran Mercedes in downtown Metropolitan Pucallpa, I was a mess. I had not bathed for several days, my clothes were stained with fish blood. I was unshaven; I stank of sweat, fish, and river mud, and I was covered from the mid-thigh with grey mud from the river. I was a normal mid-day customer at the corner café-bar of the Hotel Mercedes whose

cross-corner door opened onto the street. I asked for and was served a hot meal of catfish and bananas. Barefoot Shipibo Indian women from upriver came by my table to sell me necklaces and bracelets, but I didn't buy any.

I still have the *teote* (necklace) that Rosalia gave me that day, and I still wear it from time to time. *Uariqui shipibaopanebaquë* ("I am an adopted son of the Shipibo").

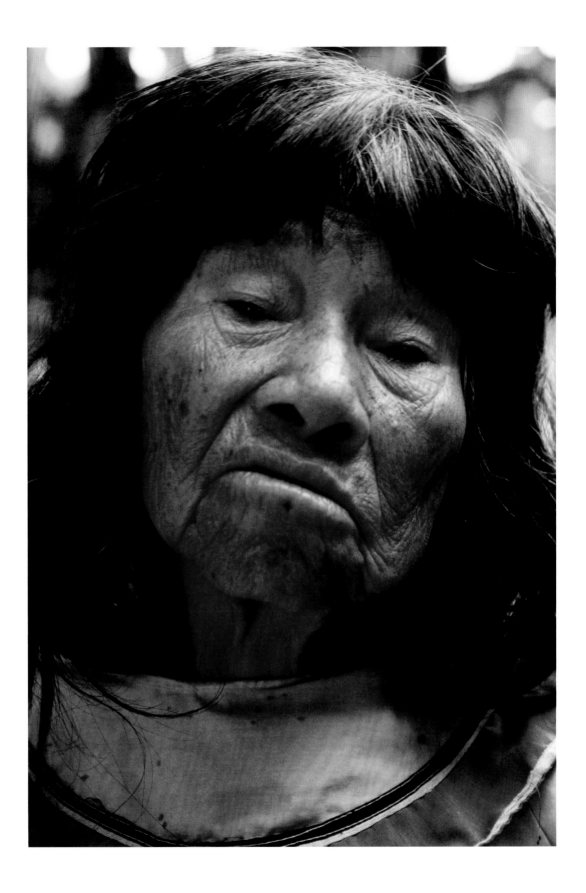

HVINITI

Huinitajahuequi
Moa shinantima

— **Shipibo proverb**

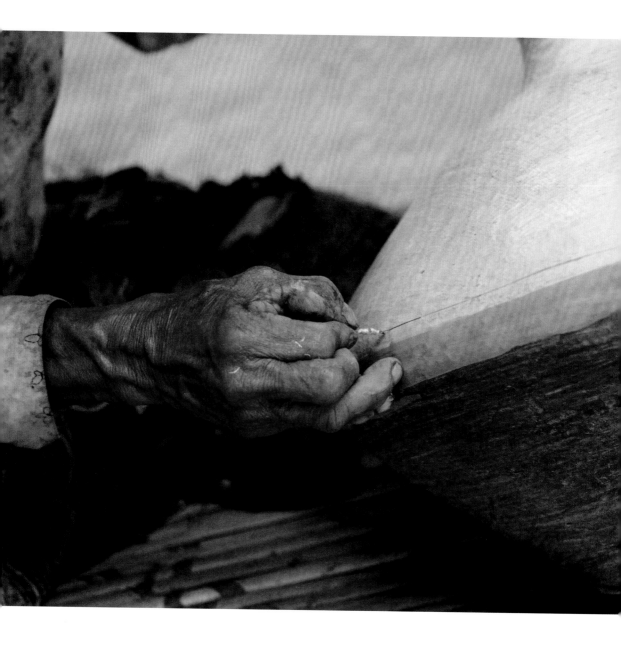

SUAVE®

SUAVE®

no es

> *mi amor cubana dice:*
> *poema no es.*

FRENCH STUDENT
OF GERMAN

I wanted to learn
the language

But when I saw the words
I was scared.

PRINCIPLES FOR SALE

Principles are expensive.

That's why so few people
Can afford them.

MR. FOO

In December 1965, when I was about half-way through my internship at Gorgas Hospital in the Canal Zone, I started my Internal Medicine rotation on the Medical Ward. One of the patients to whom I was assigned was Mr. Foo from Singapore. Mr. Foo had lung cancer.

Mr. Foo was a Chinese sailor on a merchant marine vessel that was going through the Panama Canal when he was put ashore and brought to the hospital. Mr. Foo was the ship's cook.

Gorgas Hospital, at that time, took care of all U.S. military personnel in Panama and Central and South America. All U.S. diplomatic personnel and all Peace Corps volunteers and staff from the region were brought to Gorgas if they needed medical attention. Another source of patients for Gorgas was merchant seamen who were ill while going through the Canal or in the immediate vicinity. Mr. Foo, having become ill just before his ship arrived at the Panama Canal, was brought to us and he became my patient. It was my job to visit him each day on rounds after I had reviewed his x-rays, laboratory work, and nurse's notes on his chart. The cancer in his lungs was growing steadily. His incapacity and death was only a matter of time.

By the time I saw him, Mr. Foo knew what was wrong with him. Each day I would greet him, ask him how he felt, and prepare to listen to his lungs with my stethoscope. He was unfailingly polite and reasonably cheerful. After I listened to his lungs, he would look up at me with big, mournful eyes and say, "Bad?" "Bad," I would say, nodding. Sometimes I would sit down and put my arm around his shoulder as I talked with him and asked him how he was doing.

One day, Mr. Foo showed me a letter from his son and told me that his family was in Singapore. He said he wanted to go home to see his family.

The hospital administration had a policy of flying sick merchant seamen home from the Canal Zone as soon as it was determined that they would not get well soon or if they were terminally ill. The tradition was that the intern assigned to the patient would accompany him to his destination. One of my colleagues took a guy back to Afghanistan.

There were several problems in Mr. Foo's case. One was that I was too sick to travel, as I was just recovering from infectious mononucleosis. Another problem was that the hospital had half its usual complement of interns due to the anti-American riots that had occurred in the Canal Zone the previous year. Lastly, Mr. Foo was regarded as just too sick to travel. The airlines were afraid that he would die en route. This concern was heightened by the lack of available interns to make the trip with him.

On hearing of these problems, I went to the head of the hospital, Colonel Harry Offutt, and asked for him to intercede and make the arrangements for Mr. Foo to go home without the medical chaperone. I said that he was well enough to travel now but might not be in a few weeks, and he would never see his family again or vice versa if this did not happen.

The original airline decision to transport Mr. Foo had been rescinded because of his worsening condition. Now we needed to rescind that decision.

Eventually, Mr. Foo's trip was approved. I did not see him leave because I had been assigned to a pathology rotation by that time. But several weeks later, I got a letter from Singapore:

> Foo Cheong Kam
> _____ Crescent
> Singapore, 14 (Blk 20)

> Dear Dr. Hern,

> How do you do? I am Mr. Foo Kia Wan's son. My parents told me to write this letter to thank you for your good care for him. He reached Singapore on the sixth of January and was admitted to the general hospital. He was in good condition at first, but when he fell one night in the hospital he was injected by the doctor to make him sleep so that he won't be in pain. If he had not fall, he is in good condition. Now, he rarely eats and drinks.

> The doctor here says that he had cancer in the lung. Now he is glad to be with us again. Thank you.

> Yours sincerely,
> (signed) FC Kam

INVITATION

Now a hope
A possibility of loving
Someone somewhat shy
But loving

Suddenly my heart is open
To the chill wind
The warm chinook
The gentle breeze as it may
Open to the joy and pain alike
Of loving

Will you join a passionate
Man on a mountaintop
For a starlit windswept night
For a spot by the fire
For a celebration of giving
For excursions into other nights
And spring blossoms?

Oh to touch you and feel
Your lips brush across my cheek
Your hand's gentle touch
For that moment too brief

I cannot wait quietly
Until you join me.

SMALL MEADOW

We were married
In a meadow
On a hill in Colorado
Under the gold aspen leaves
Surrounded by the love
Of those we love
But not everyone we love
Small meadow

THE PRICE
OF MY LOVE

Don't pretend to be my friend.

You have exacted from me
What my love is worth to you.

Not much.

Learning that, I have concluded
That is more than I can afford.

GREAT BRINGER OF DEATH
TO PARADISE

Crossing the creek on a log
I look down to steady myself
The water runs deep and clear
Below it
So cool to drink
Nothing better in the world

I am going to a place unknown
And then to a place in the past
To see the truth of what is gone
And what is there
To know
To feel the pain
To see the work of The Great
Bringer of Death to Paradise

The bank is steep
The thicket hides the stepping place
Each step an act of faith
Takes all my strength
The mountain doesn't care

The pass rises out of the bowl
Bottomed by a blue lake
Serene and bewildered
Not knowing it is wild

I watch the sky
For that sudden lethal crackle
Creeping greyly across
From cliff to cliff
As I creep slowly pantingly painfully
Across the littered careless stones
I'm lightning bait

Down down down the other side
There's a lake there's two
That's not the one I'm heading for
I'm heading for another and yet
A ravaged place beyond

Now I find a quiet place and find
A bluff to look out
To see the splendid mountains
And the monument to greed

A fish is hungry
I am fed
A cannibal fish full of unsmelt eggs
Yet another, native noble prey
Blazed with courage colors of the fall

Shall I go or stay and rest
Enjoy the comfort of this cool spot
Down down down I go
Down a cliff to the valley's floor
To see the wretched remains
Of what I knew

Rocks bleached bones
Skeletons shorn of tops
Grey stumps and sparse mud
Death has come to paradise

Beneath the half filled crater
In the memory only lies
Meadows brooks beaver works
Trickles ponds tall grass
Ooze
A boy's dreams
A father's loving teaching
Weather and time working its ways
To make a carpet for the living

Death has come to paradise
Untimely death as so 'tis said
Before the universe winds down
The Bringer of Death to Paradise
Impatient takes his toll

Back to the tattered remains
Of paradise
A quiet lake so quiet
Hear your heart
Body working to stay alive
Each chipmunk squeak each chirp
Each note of every bird
Every ripple of the lake

Up there on the mountainside
Somewhere in the timber
Coyotes' shimmering falsetto
Echoes down the mountainside
Splashing off the rocks in a
Waterfall of rippling sound

A primeaval chorus to the mountain gods
A howl from the jungle
An animal togetherness
We are here

To know their language
I would give much

A golden brown hungry trout
Old long fat knowing where to look
Mouth open wide for prey
Prowls the shallow end of my lake
Mine only for a moment
One small trout swirls all the water
In that glassy lake
He will survive there
Does he know more than I?

Morning sun shines through
The velvet of two bucks' horns
They quietly step up on up
The steep mountain above me
And disappear

What is this strange creature
That advances on us
Making these wheezing gurgling sounds?

If deer can think
What would they think?

Resting looking down
I am still for a moment
The bucks emerge
Browsing looking relaxing tense again
Hold my breath don't move
They watch me then
Go about their browse
Atop the pass another omen
A hawk just overhead
Wings steady
Not a sound but wind
He's gone

There by a tundra pond
A lone coyote stalks hops pounces
Back the other way
To catch his quarry
Has his prey
Rips and tears
Head lifting up each time
Satisfied lies down
And licks himself

What is the world's trouble
To a coyote?

Only if he is in the way
Of the Great Bringer of Death
To Paradise
Death is coming to paradise.

CIVILIZATION . . . OR PREDATOR?

IT WAS 1950 when my father took me to Homestake Lake for the first time. I was twelve. We pitched camp near the old mining cabins at Gold Park. After rising at dawn and countering the morning chill with a hot breakfast over a campfire, we gathered our fishing tackle and started across the meadow. The trail crossed small brooks and took us up along a roaring, tumbling Homestake Creek.

Surely, Homestake was one of the most beautiful streams in the world for that stretch. There were deep holes and many waterfalls. We would stop to rest, drink a little of that wonderfully clear water, watch the trout, and enjoy being there together.

My father has said he felt closer to God there than in any church. He is not a religious man, but there with him by the creek and lake I learned of reverence for life.

Homestake Lake, the meadows and beaver dams on beyond, and the stream that flowed from it, were places that I grew to love. It was my first experience with real wilderness, a place of solitude and great beauty. I wanted my ashes to be scattered there above the lake when I died.

After high school, I didn't go back. I was away learning my profession and learning about the rest of the world. Homestake Lake was always going to be there, and I would go back someday. I knew I would take my own children so they could experience the mysteries and power of nature.

In 1975, it was too late. A dam had been built across Homestake Valley just below the lake. I had heard about it, but I didn't want to see it. I hiked that fall with a friend into East Cross Creek instead. After coming out and starting home, I turned back anyway to see what had happened to Homestake. I was apprehensive.

Some of the beaver dams and brooks were dry. Part of the lower meadow was there, but the wild stream was still. A sterile, ugly dam crossed the valley. The lake and wilderness that I loved had been transformed into an irrigation ditch.

There was nothing left to do but cry, and I did.

Perhaps a boy's love of the woods is not really important. Perhaps the opportunity for parents to be with their children alone in a place where the

natural world surrounds the senses with uncorrupted beauty is not important. But suppose these things are important, after all.

Suppose we discover that reverence for the web of life is not only important but vital to our survival as a species. Suppose that it is more important even than real estate values and development and bluegrass lawns and city council elections.

Having glimpsed that possibility, we must recognize in the destruction of Homestake a loss of inestimable value.

A civilization that can no longer preserve its places of sanctuary and beauty is no longer a civilization but a mindless predator.

VALUES CLASH OVER WILD WATERS

By Warren M. Hern

THERE IS NO PLACE THAT SYMBOLIZES COLORADO more than the Holy Cross Wilderness. Its towering peaks and waterfalls, tumbling creeks, quiet meadows with meandering streams, carpets of wildflowers, and abundant wildlife are at the core of those things that make Colorado a special place. It is a rare and beautiful national treasure.

The Holy Cross Wilderness is being threatened, however, by the greed of Aurora and Colorado Springs developers and by the obstinacy of those cities' public officials.

Homestake I, a water diversion project built by those cities in the 1960s, destroyed Homestake Valley by turning it into a bomb crater. The tunnels leading from the Homestake Dam have collapsed numerous times. By itself, Homestake I is a gigantic boondoggle. The only way to salvage it, as well as the careers of the officials who planned it, is to build another boondoggle: Homestake II.

Homestake II would put eleven miles of tunnels under the Mount of the Holy Cross and other ridges in the heart of the Holy Cross Wilderness. Diversion dams would then suck the wilderness nearly dry.

The project would remove up to 95 percent of the water from the area's major streams during peak runoff. The wetlands would dry out. The crashing waterfalls downstream would become trickles. The developers would get their profit and the water bureaucrats could put their names on another monument to stupidity.

A Denver federal court decision on the project in July strikes another blow against the wilderness and brings Colorado water wars to a boil again.

Two important issues of public policy are at stake in the decision: whether Colorado's Front Range cities can continue to dry up large areas of the Western Slope to fuel Front Range development, and whether federal agencies charged with protecting the wilderness areas can be required to make sound decisions.

   64

The answer to the first question is "yes," since there is no suitable mechanism for stopping the diversions. The answer to the second question, unfortunately, is "no." The courts have given the agencies in this case a blank check.

The lowest possible standard is now being applied to the agency decisions about the environmental impacts of obviously destructive projects. In her opinion, Judge Zita Weinshienk ruled that decisions by the U.S. Forest Service and the U.S. Army Corps of Engineers to permit construction of the Homestake II water project, even though based on "inadequate and inaccurate" information, could not be found to be "arbitrary and capricious."

The consequence of the court's ruling, which followed U.S. Supreme Court precedents, is that a federal agency may make decisions affecting the environment that are stupid and incompetent, but the decisions must stand if they are made deliberately.

The decision is a setback in the decade-long battle to save the Holy Cross Wilderness from the ravages of the water developers. (Officials of Aurora and Colorado Springs, while admitting that they have up to twice as much water as they need, insist on building the $250 million project to prove "it can be done.") Hydrologists and biologists consulted by the Holy Cross Wilderness Defense Fund have shown that the project's removal of 20,000 acre-feet of water per year would cause irreversible damage to the wetlands below the diversion points.

The cities' plan is to connect tunnels from the existing Homestake I project to water diversion structures high in the wilderness. The water in the streams there would empty into the tunnels and be pumped to the Eastern Slope. The water could end up costing almost ten times as much as that obtained by the cities from other sources.

In 1986, David Cooper, an ecologist hired by the Defense Fund, collected two rare plants growing in the wilderness. Both would be affected by the water diversion and one, a peat moss growing in the wetlands, would be wiped out by the changes. Consultants for both the Corps of Engineers and the cities agree that large areas of the wetlands below the diversions—up to 240 acres—would be affected by the loss of spring runoff water.

A fundamental problem with both the federal agency permits and the court decision is that the agencies issued the permits before ordering a baseline study of the wilderness ecosystem. The study, conducted at a cost of one million dollars by the sponsoring cities, was not completed until four years after the last permit was issued.

After providing information that showed the drop in water levels would seriously affect the wilderness wetlands, the study concluded that there would be no serious effect. Experts reviewing the document stated that it was so poorly done its results could not be published in a scientific journal.

Yet the decision in July means there is no effective judicial review of either the U.S. Forest Service's or the Corps of Engineers' observance of the federal laws under which the permits to build Homestake II were issued.

Even if the permits stand after appeal, they contain the seeds of futility for the Homestake II project. The permit issued by the Corps of Engineers states that any change in the wetlands following initiation of water diversion will result in immediate cessation of the diversion. Unless someone in the cities' utility departments has single-handedly reversed the law of gravity, photosynthesis and the process of ecological succession, the wetlands will change. The cities will own a $250 million hole in the ground.

The fight over Homestake II is fundamentally about values. It is a question of whether bluegrass lawns, clean cars, and real estate profits are more important than delicate Pink Fairy Slipper Orchids growing on the banks of a mountain torrent, the majesty of a thundering wilderness waterfall, the spectacle of

hundreds of thousands of wildflowers nodding in the breeze, the safety of a Colorado cutthroat trout hiding under a moss bank, the freedom of a beaver pushing its branch through a flooded channel, or the view of an unnamed mountain range across the open solitude of a mountain meadow.

We must choose. We have already destroyed too much of the Colorado that had these things. An important part of it remains in the Holy Cross Wilderness.

Dr. Warren M. Hern is chairman of the board of the Holy Cross Wilderness Defense Fund in Boulder.

THE STAGES OF MAN

Organization
for survival

       Organization
       for exploitation

              Organization
                     for survival

READING COPY

THANK YOU FOR BEING HERE TO BE WITNESSES FOR PEACE AND TO HONOR THE MEMORY OF THOSE WHO HAVE DIED FOR OUR FREEDOM.

I ALSO WANT TO THANK THE ORGANIZERS OF THIS WONDERFUL EVENT AND MY FRIENDS ON THE PLATFORM WHO ARE ALSO SPEAKING OUT FOR FREEDOM.

FREEDOM IS IN TROUBLE IN AMERICA. THE RIGHT OF WOMEN TO CHOOSE AND TO BE SAFE IS IN DANGER. THE ATTACK ON THAT RIGHT TO CHOOSE IS A WEAPON TO DESTROY FREEDOM FOR EVERYONE. WE MUST RESIST THIS ATTACK.

THE PEOPLE OF BOULDER LOVE FREEDOM, AND BOULDER IS THE MOST PRO-CHOICE COMMUNITY IN THE COUNTRY. BUT THE NATIONAL TERRORIST ANTI-ABORTION MOVEMENT AFFECTS ALL OF US. UNWELCOME, IT TOUCHES US IN BOULDER.

WE MUST NOW ASK: CAN A DOCTOR WHO DOES LEGAL ABORTIONS WALK FOR A FEW BLOCKS FROM HIS OFFICE WITHOUT AN ARMED ESCORT TO A PUBLICLY ANNOUNCED PEACEFUL ASSEMBLY IN THIS PUBLIC PLACE TO SPEAK TO YOU, HIS FELLOW CITIZENS, WITHOUT A SERIOUS RISK OF BEING ASSASSINATED BY THOSE WHO HATE FREEDOM?

THE ANSWER, MY FRIENDS, IS "NO." THINK ABOUT WHAT THAT MEANS FOR YOUR COUNTRY.

73

CAN MY JEWISH FRIEND AND COLLEAGUE IN DENVER, ALSO A DOCTOR WHO DOES ABORTIONS, GO TO HIS SYNAGOGUE WITH HIS FAMILY TO WORSHIP HIS GOD IN PEACE WITHOUT INDECENT HARASSMENT BY ANTI-ABORTION FANATICS ? THE ANSWER IS "NO."

IS IT POSSIBLE THAT A DOCTOR WHO HAS SPENT HIS LIFE HELPING WOMEN AND THEIR FAMILIES, WHO HAS A DISTIN-GUISHED CAREER AS A PHYSICIAN AND EDUCATOR, MIGHT BE DENIED AN OPPORTUNITY TO SERVE AS OUR NATION'S PUBLIC HEALTH LEADER JUST BECAUSE HE HAS ALSO DONE SOME ABORTIONS TO SAVE WOMEN'S LIVES? THE ANSWER TO THAT QUESTION IS "YES."

THE ANSWERS TO THESE QUESTIONS MEAN THAT FREEDOM IS IN TROUBLE IN AMERICA, NOT JUST FOR WOMEN, BUT FOR EVERYONE. WE MUST WIN OUR FREEDOM EVERY DAY AGAINST THE FORCES OF IGNORANCE, FEAR, REACTION, AND TYRANNY.

WE WILL.

-30-30-30-

PAIN

Sometimes
The only thing
You can do
With real pain

Is to embrace it.

It's part of you.

WITH YOU

When I am with you,
That's where I want to be.
There is no other more desired destination,
No other place I would rather be.

When I am with you,
I am most alive;
My life is happening.
There is joy in your presence.

Pain lurks, but it is at bay
In the shadows.

When I am with you,
I forget the pain
Stalking snarling in the shadows.

Are you a drug?
I want more.

Loving you is the essence of my life,
The elixir of eternity
And the instant moment.
Your laughter is my sustenance,
Your loving touch, electric.
I am a bundle of protons
Seeking to know your nucleus,
Your center,
Without the swirling layers that conceal it.

In between those moments,
I think of you
And enjoy the lingering joy
Of your caress
And the vision of your eyes alive.

Would that these things were also true
For you.

PARAWEASEL

The paraweasel scurries
Through the shadows
Of the sewer of evil
In the valley of death

Furtive eyes darting
Looking for a soft spot
A vulnerable outcrop of truth
Stalking freedom
With a dagger
Of rotten rolled up paper

Bubonic plague is banished
But not the paraweasel
Or a plague of lies and fear
Of threats of death
Of strangling of liberty
Twisting truth
To suffocate the spirit
Darkness sweeps over us

Resistance braces us
Against the fear the moving shadows
the sleepless anxious nights
Bringing the light
Paraweasel squeaks and scurries
Back into the shadows
For awhile

NOTE FROM
A PATIENT

thank you
for
giving me back
my life

CIVILIZATION

the veneer of civilization
is very thin

and a lot of people
are out there

trying to scrape it off

FUCKING ABOUT

You want to have a kid
I want to have a kid
Here we are having tea

Life is exploding
Life is running out

It's worth thinking about
It's worth talking about

Is it worth fucking about?

THE NINETIES WOMAN

look but don't touch
touch but don't feel
feel but not too much

heel
sit
beg
lie down

give me your sperm

go away.

LIFE AND DEATH

I am not afraid
To die.

I am afraid
Of not having lived.

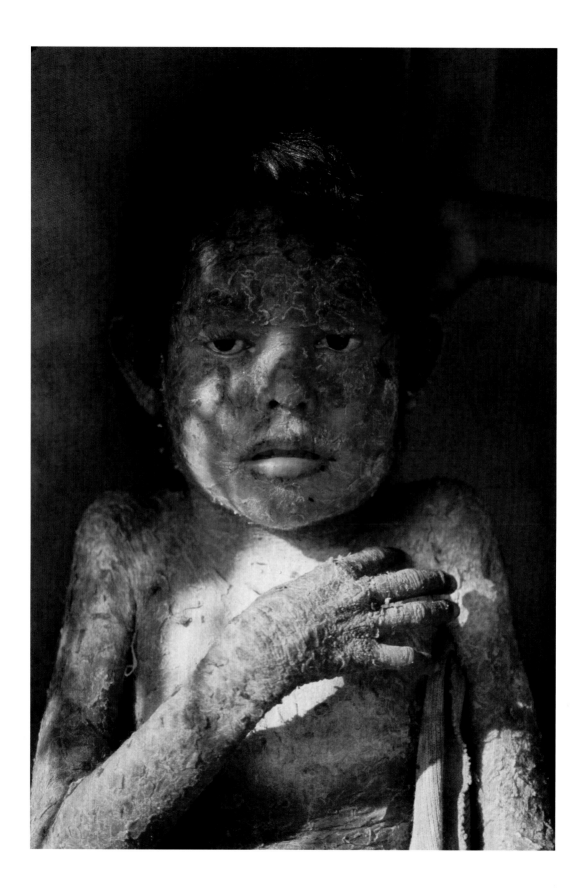

NUEVE DE OCTUBRE

THE LOWER PISQUI RIVER has had a reputation as a bad and uncomfortable place for a long time. Early explorers described the plight of some hapless Jesuit missionaries who attempted to go up the Pisqui during the rainy season one time in the late eighteenth century. They entered the mouth of the Pisqui from the Ucayali River, which is about ten kilometers wide at that point in the rainy season, and they found themselves in a bewildering maze of false channels, lagoons, tangled swamps, and walls of vegetation. Staying in the main channel is a good idea, but it isn't always possible.

The missionaries were miserable, to put it mildly. There was no dry land, no place to seek or improvise a shelter, no dry wood for a fire, no fish to catch as the fish were all in the flooded underbrush, no game to shoot for meat because there was no ground for animals to walk on, and utter darkness at night. The mosquitoes were voracious. Finally, the Pisquibo (Shipibo from the Pisqui River villages) found the missionaries and put them out of their misery. It was a long time before other missionaries tried the Pisqui again.

The first main village on the Pisqui that we encountered on our first trip up that river was Nuevo de octubre (Ninth of October). The village contained about forty-eight people, more or less, and some of them were friendly. One of the most remarkable things about the environment was the clouds of mosquitoes, especially in the evening and at dawn, although there was never a time when there weren't many. They were huge. It was amazing that any human being could survive their predation.

Fortunately, my small canoe had some planks for a narrow deck and tin roof that made it possible to sleep under a mosquito net on the boards instead of under worse conditions.

The village contained one large extended family. The great-grandparents lived at the downstream end of the village. Three of their daughters were the wives of one man, who was the nominal leader of the village. He was a quiet, thin, gentle man who was respectful and helpful, and he was grateful for the medicine we brought. Each of his three wives had her own pole-and-thatch house with attached kitchen, a covered area for a cooking fire. Each of his wives had several children, some of them adult with their own children.

About five meters behind the middle house was a little hut about two by three meters on a side and about two meters high. It had a dirt floor and a cot made of poles. Inside was Silvia, who was ten years old. She was covered with scales and sores, her skin flaking off her entire body. Her father spoke to her softly and gently, bringing her food and water, bathing her, and helping her with her toilet. She was naked most of the time except at night when it was cold. She

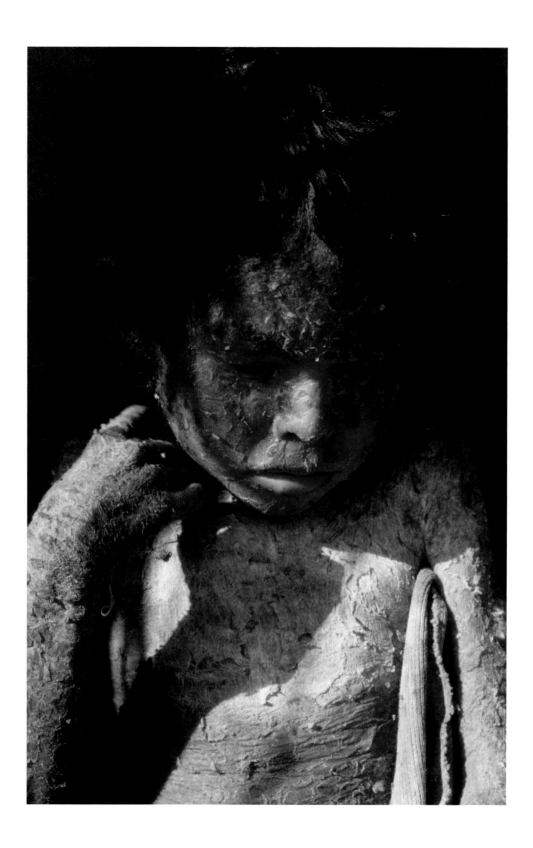

made no sound. She looked at me with eyes of great suffering. She was ashamed, but her father told her that I was a doctor and was there to help her.

I did not know what was wrong with Silvia, but I had seen several children and one adult with something like this from time to time in other villages. When I was a medical student working with Dr. Binder in 1964 at the Hospital Amazonico "Albert Schweitzer," he had shown me a Campa child with what he called "pemphigus," a condition I found identified as "pemphigus vulgaris" in one of the medical books in the hospital library. The child had large blisters that Dr. Binder treated with steroids. According to Silvia's father, her illness had started this way. In another village up the Ucayali from the Pisqui, I had one time seen another child with this condition whose blisters had broken, were bleeding, and had become infected.

My first thought was that Silvia might have some nutritional deficiency brought about an overwhelming burden of intestinal parasites, but I had no way of really making a diagnosis. But I thought it would not hurt her to treat her for parasites, since all Shipibo children had them, and it might help her. So I started her on several courses of anti-parasitic medications, and I gave her vitamins in case her hideous affliction was the result of a vitamin deficiency disease.

One month later, when we stopped to spend the night before going on down to the Ucayali and starting the long trip up that river, Silvia seemed a little better. Her father said her appetite was better.

An influenza epidemic came through the villages on the Pisqui a few weeks later. Silvia died.

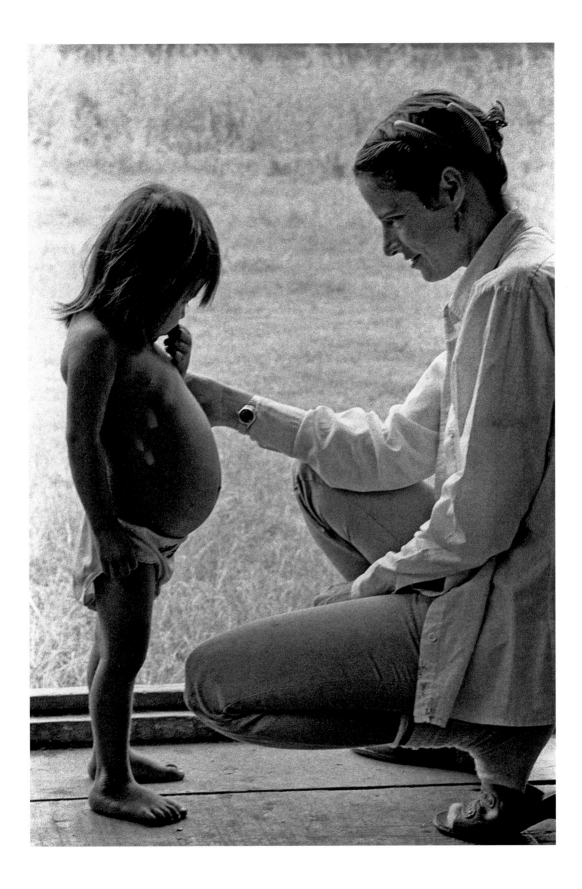

FLOWER

you are a

    flower

        of a person

YOUR VOICE

To me,

your voice

is the sweetest sound

in the world.

THE WOW

love is what's left

after the wow is gone

TRANSMISSION

Observation:
Your thing is floppy,
Even when it's in gear.

Response:
You really know how
To hurt a guy.

LETTER FROM NUEVO EDEN

CAIBIMA

PAOYHAN CC. NN.   RIO UCAYALI

19 November 1990
Nuevo Edén, Peru

Dear PJ:

This is just a short note to let you know what is happening
and where i am. There is a boat leaving for Pucallpa tomorrow
and i am sending a man with appendicitis on it so he can be
operated on.   i will be surprised if he survives. One of
the leaders of the community is going on the boat and I am sending
this letter with him. I hope you get it.

We left Pao two weeks ago this Wednesday. Two days out, the
support bracket for the rudder and propeller began to disintegrate.
We got from one village to another by borrowing equipment. We
finally got one we could keep for our trip while mine was being
fixed, but that one, too, began to develop problems. The rest
of the trip up to this village was held together literally by
about 5 cents worth of jute cord. It took us five days to get
here. This is the place I was thrown out of in 1984. Now
they are desperate and I am welcome. The study isgoing reasonably
well, but the people sre almost too sick to study. The place is
one big emergency room. It is a beautiful place with the
Cordillera Azul rizing abruptly out of the jungle a few miles
away, and there is still quite a bit of wildlife here. One of
my men was almost bitten by a large poisonous snake by the river
this afternoon. I have made soup out of whats left of our
chunk of a sajino (a collared peccary) that one of the
men killed while fishing the other day. I am in good health,
feasting on fresh wild pig, fresh roasted bananans, and
fresh roasted peanuts (native to the Amazon), with fresh pineapple
for dessert. The people are wonderful, although not uniformly
so. The research is going well, but slowly. There are several
polygynous families here that i have wanted to study for many
years, and i am finally getting to do it. I plan to spend until
the end of this week here then move on to the next village down
the river. Things are going more or less as planned.

I would like to stay here for six months or so, but since that
is impossible, i will settle for two weeks.

This village in most ways is much more the old Shipibo culture
than anyplace I have worked, although in other ways it is more
modern. What I am seeing is the transition from isolated local
tribal life to integration, for better or worse (I think worse)
in the national economy. For example, the people are participating
in the logging activities in the headwaters where the ecological
destruction has the most impact and is irreversible. It will
destroy their entire way of life and they will be left without
anything. They are just starting thepattern that has destroyed
many Amazon cultures.

On the good side, an old woman in the village with whom I was
having a spirited if somewhat incomplete conversation in Shipibo
decided that i am all right and adopted me on the spot, so I
have been adopted now in several villages. It is an honor.

My best to everyone,

P.S. It rained all night in a terrific thunderstorm so hard you
can't believe it can rain that hard, enough to make your ears
ring, and most of the day, so the river is now rising about a
meter an hour and we may be in a lake tomorrow. So the current
is very fast and the letter will get there sooner. I have my
crew conducting experiments tomorrow to calculate the velocity
of the river current in the Pisqui. Stay tuned.

NEGOTIABILITY

Observation:
Everything is negotiable.

Response:
Some things are not negotiable.

THE WEED
IN YOUR GARDEN

As one of the weeds
In your garden
Who escaped (or maybe I didn't)
I'd like to know
What it's like
Not to be weeded out

Better yet
What it's like
Not to be a weed.

TOO MUCH SCHOOL

Sitting on the weight bench
Sweating
Taking a breather
In between sets and reps
Pumpin' 'em up
Feeling fit
But need a break
In the college gym

Surrounded by machismo
Hot bodies
Testosterone poisoning
Girlfriends getting "help"

Shyly, softly, sweetly
She sits down carefully across from me
Very young
Cautious
Looks the other way
Finally says,

Are you a graduate student?

Yes, how did you know?

A moment's hesitation
Not knowing quite what to say next
Respectfully, she replies

You look like you've had
A lot of school.

SILENCIO

La casa es vacio,
Hay silencio,
La cama es fria, y
Te echo de menos.
Te amo

DIAMOND LOVER

Tu eres
una amante
diamante.

WORKING ON BREAD

Are you still working
on the bread, sir?
asked the waiter

No, I said
I am *eating* the bread.

INTELLIGENT DESIGN

CREATIONISM

What's intelligent about this design?

How can the Dover School Board advocates of the magical theory of creation-ism maintain that there is an intelligent design(er) of the universe when this process has resulted in the ascension of George W. Bush to the presidency of the United States? There is nothing intelligent about that. But then, maybe this disproves the theory of evolution, also. We have gone from Demosthenes to Dubya.

> —Warren M. Hern
> Boulder

SPIROAGNOSIS

Sirs:

I have enjoyed my new subscription to *The New Republic* and found it particularly informative during the recent fall election campaign. This was especially helpful since, as duly noted in the columns of your journal, we were subjected to an inordinate amount of nonsense and foolishness from all sides. As an epidemiologist, I cannot help noting that this is a mass phenomenon with acute exacerbations and remissions.

Being a sometime Greek scholar, I followed a hunch, thinking that perhaps the names of those engaged in these activities might provide clues as to the nature of the malady. Greek has always offered us a wealth of definitions for use in medical terminology, so I naturally began with the name of a recently obscure but now leading politician of Greek extraction who has become one of the more prominent purveyors of political perversity.

Consulting my copy of Liddell and Scott's abridged *Greek-English Lexicon* (Oxford Press, 1958), I found the word *speiro* on page 645 defined as "to scatter like seed, fling, throw about: to spread a report." Page 6 was even more informative:

agnoéo—not to perceive or know, to be ignorant
ágnoiá—a want of perception, ignorance
agnomonéo—to act without judgement, act ignorantly or unfairly
agnomónos—senselessly
agnomosúnei—want of sense or judgment, senseless pride, arrogance
agnós—unknown, obscure. Obscure, ignoble, not knowing, ignorant of.
agnosía—a not-knowing, ignorance. A being unknown, obscurity.

These definitions, while imprecise in themselves, offer us a clear enough juxtaposition of similar meanings to allow identification of this affliction. I suggest we call it "spiroagnosis," meaning, "to go around spreading nonsense."

The diagnosis of this illness is simple. Its principal victims exhibit hyperventilation, mandibular fibrillation, and the spouting of patent nonsense. Alliteration is a common finding. The secondary attack rate is high, particularly when the audiences are large and well supplied with expensive liquor.

The treatment is long, painful, and difficult, consisting mainly of education.

The prognosis is excellent if preventive treatment is instituted early in life, but most untreated cases appear to be intractable and quite hopeless once the process has become established.

—Warren M. Hern, M.D.
Washington, D.C.

BANQUET OF CRUMBS

I offer you a banquet
And you complain
About the arrangement
Of the crumbs
Under the table.

CZECH POINT

Observation (Czech woman):
Why do all the women on this trail
Have several huge dogs with them?

Response (American man):
For protection.

Pause.

Comment (Czech woman):
They don't need it.

CREATURE OF YOUR HEART'S DESIRE

I am/have become
A creature of your heart's desire

I yearn to be
Your dream and ecstasy
As you have become mine

JE T'AIME

Je m'endors pensant à toi

Je me réveille pensant à toi

Tous les jours, je pense à toi

Je t'aime.

WHAT IS POETRY?

When is a tangle of words
A poem?

When you think it is, I guess

When is a poem not a poem?

When you are deconstructed
Instead of completely unreconstructed

I guess

"IF YOU'RE A GOOD AMERICAN, STAND UP!"

By Warren Hern and Dan Nickelson

Churchgoers

Warren Hern and Dan Nickelson took a trip down to Denver recently to go to "church" after seeing an ad in a Denver newspaper advertising a sermon on Americanism with a free movie thrown in—*Operation Abolition*. Hern is a fifth-year student with a distributed major. Nickelson is a senior political science major.

"If you're a Good American, stand up!"

The people rise from their seats. "Amen." "Glory." "Praise God!" You are afraid to turn your head to see. The choir is marching up the side aisle in step to the strains of *The Battle Hymn of the Republic*. Each choir member carries a hymnal and a tiny American flag. They march to the chancel and past a single-standard row of six American flags. Across from these, another solid row of flags.

You notice a movement to your left; a file of boys in Boy Scout uniforms present the flag to the congregation. The speaker begins the Pledge of Allegiance, and while you are saying it you notice the boys' uniforms. They are not Boy Scout uniforms, for each has a sleeve-stripe at the shoulder. The youngest uniformed boy looks about four years old.

After the Pledge of Allegiance, more patriotic hymns accompanied by a very bad but very loud trombone. Suddenly you notice a man in front of you to your left. His eyes are closed, his fists clenched, his arms moving in time to the music, his head shaking in ecstasy. The music stops, and he cheers and claps. The people sit down. "Praise be to God!" "Amen." "That's right brother!" The man you were watching turns nervously to look at you, looking up and down looking scared. He turns back, begins to chew on his fingernails. The loudspeaker startles you, blaring, "Are you a Good American? Stand up if you are!"

The city: Denver, 1961. The scene: a non-denominational "church." The atmosphere: strikingly similar to the ritualistic settings shown in the propaganda films of recent authoritarian political movements.

The loudspeaker screams at you, drowning every other sensation; you are reminded of the "Two-Minute Hate" in Orwell's *1984*. The speaker is saying, "America for Americans for America!" He screams accusingly, "There are Communists here tonight . . . right now! We know you're here!"

You are afraid to move, afraid to look away from the speaker, afraid to cough lest the speaker seize upon your action as proof of black sin. The speaker waves a large Bible, quotes J. Edgar Hoover, pours Hell-fire and damnation on "You . . . you . . . you . . . ." "That's right, brother!" "Oh, Lord!" "GOD SAVE US!"

The man in the next row has his eyes closed again, cheering and striking the air before him. The speaker's voice becomes quiet. He says, "We believe in freedom of opinion, freedom of speech. We believe in the American Way of Life. We hate COMMUNISTS!" "Amen." "That's right, brother."

His voice rises. "If you aren't an American and for America, we're AGAINST you!" "If you don't agree with us, GET OUT OF THE COUNTRY!"

The man with the hyperthyroid eyes turns to look at you over his shoulder. You cringe, look away, try to appear calm. He turns back to his ecstasy, and you relax a little, but you feel like turning up your collar to hide the back of your neck.

"If a teacher won't pledge allegiance to the flag of America, he shouldn't teach your children . . . he should be RUN OUT!" "Praise God!" "That's RIGHT, brother!" ". . . America for Americans for America!" "Glory!" "Amen."

After the shouting speech, a collection is taken. You're in the second row of the middle section. The plate comes to you already heaped with five- and ten-dollar bills. You furtively put in some loose change. You look up to see the man in the next row staring at you, his eyes wide, nervous, suspicious. You look down, away, anything to avoid his glace, knowing he will jump up any second and shout, "He's a COMMUNIST!"

Finally, they show the film you came to see—*Operation Abolition*. The crowd reacts as before, cheering the police and booing the students, laughing when a demonstrator is washed down the steps.

After the film, a different speaker takes the platform. He works up the crowd to a frenzy again, but you notice he is less effective than the first speaker. He tells of a group they will be organizing on nearby college campuses. The group will be called "The Student Patriots of America."

"We will start a newspaper," he says. The newspaper will be called *The Student Patriot*. The speaker tells the people it will take $5,000 to start the newspaper and college organizations. "Who is a Good American? Stand up. Who is a Good American who will pledge $100 tonight for this cause?"

One man stands up, then another, and another. Finally, no more respond. "Who is a good American who will pledge $50 tonight?" The speaker works down to $25, to $10, to $5, to $1, and then he and the first speaker start going through the audience, row by row, collecting $1 and $5 bills.

When we got outside, we estimated that the second speaker had received over $850 in pledges, not counting the offering before this film and the row-by-row collection afterwards. Not bad . . . not bad at all.

As we started back to Boulder, we were sobered by what we had just seen. Why? Why do these people turn to demagogues? Why do they let themselves be used? Why are these demagogues so effective? Why do people surrender themselves to blind, mindless hate? Why the strange alliance of religion and super-patriotism? We came to no definite conclusions, but many things became clear as we discussed the experience.

The speakers had alternatively played on feelings loyalty, rivalry, conformity . . . but most of all, fear. The people are afraid, but powerless to act. They feel insignificant in a mass society, confronted with inscrutable forces while cut off from any immediate means of dealing with those forces. They feel threatened, but they are not sure what threatens them.

The speakers directed this diffuse fear toward a faceless ogre, a scapegoat on which the people could focus their emotional energies. With it the "ministers" coupled an authoritarian religious attitude drawing the people into a masochistic feeling of blind, selfless submersion in a pseudo "loyalty," a perverted devotion, an ultra-nationalism.

The "in-group" appeal was strong, expressing overt hostility to all "foreigners" and persons of different opinions. Absent in the tirade was any rational analysis of communism as an ideology or movement. Not one word was spoken about the effects of communism on individuals or groups.

No rational exposition whatever was made of the ways of dealing with communism in actual situations.

The main argument against communism was that it is "Godless and atheistic." After all, God is on our side. Ours is the Truth, the Way, and the Life. We noticed also an almost conscious effort on the part of the "ministers" to obscure thought and foster blind obedience.

What are the consequences? What does this do to our society? We shudder to think of what might be in store.

During the Conference on World Affairs, Henry Steele Commager pointed out that nationalism throughout the world is becoming more and more militant while our problems are increasingly global in nature. It is clear that we, as leaders of the "free world," cannot afford to become more nationalistic. We cannot afford to draw into ourselves. Yet it seems to be happening.

The kind of attitude and hysteria described here can only destroy us from within by dissipating our energies on mutual suspicion. It can only choke our efforts to deal with communism on an effective basis in the rice paddies, deserts, and jungles across the world.

We might call it "The new hypnosis," for it paralyzes thought, abolishes the individual, and fills the vacuum with a political trance. It is the old totalitarianism with new fixtures. Don't say with the aristocrats of the '30s that "it can't happen here," because it could happen here.

UN VIAGGIO INTERESSANTE CON UNA CONCLUSIONE SORPRENDENTE E PIACEVOLE

di
Sr. Warren M. Hern
Fiorentino di Adozione
1 maggio 1996

QUESTO RACCONTO È SUL MIO VIAGGIO *in Italia in aprile dell'anno scorso. Questo viaggio era la prima volta in Italia. Prima, io ho visitato Firenze, dove ho partecipato a un congresso internazionale di antropologia e demografia.*

Il congresso si temevo in un posto antico e storico, il Palazzo Nonfinito vicino al Duomo e al Bargello. Durante una settimana a Firenze, ho visitato la città di Siena. Ho anche visitato la Galleria degli Uffizi. Nell' Ácademia, ho visto la scultura David *fatta dal fiorentino Michelangelo. Ho visitato Il Palazzo dei Medici e alcune sculture.*

Alle sera, io sono uscito con amici ad ascoltare concerti di musica per organo, opera, musica da camera, jazz, e tutti i tipi di musica. Ci sono anche molti buoni ristoranti a Firenze, e ho cenato in alcuni.

Il sabato dopo il congresso, ho camminato fino a Fiesole, una distanza di dieci kilometri piu o meno, e sono ritornato camminando per un'altra via. Mi piaceva molto parlare con la gente durante il cammino, vedere i posti e i palazzi antichi.

Non appena sono arrivato a Fiesole, la prima cosa che ho udito era musica sacra per organo. Subito ho scoperto che ero arrivato dietro alla cattedrale principale di Fiesole. Entrando nella cattedrale, ho udito musica di Bach (Toccata e fuga in Re minore) *suonata dal maestro di musica della cattedrale.*

Durante la seconda settimana, sono andato in automobile a Lucca, Pisa, San Gimignano, Volterra, Monteriggioni, Perugia, e altre cittadine Toscane. Mi piace molto la Toscana e la gente Toscana. Per sostenermi durante il viaggio, ho comprato vino da tavola, pane, formaggio pecorino (ho già una dedizione fatale a questo formaggio), salsiccia di cinghiale, e un coltello per tagliare le cose. Il coltello l'ho comprato in Colle Val d'Elsa, il posto di una famosa battaglia. Ma non ho comprato il coltello quí perché voglio combattere ma perché avevo fame.

Alle fine della seconda settimana, sono andato a Venezia in treno. Ho pernottato in un hotel al Lido lontano dall parte principale (centro) di Venezia. Felicemente, mi piace molto viaggare in nave.

La sera del mio primo giorno a Venezia, mi sono divertito a un concerto di Vivaldi alla Scuola Grande di San Rocco, un palazzo bellissimo. Il giorno dopo, ho fatto una passegiata in gondola per Venezia. Ho mangiato cucina eccellente nel ristorante Donna Maria vicino al Ponte Rialto. Sopra il Ponte Rialto, ho comprato tre cravatte italiane.

Dopo il mio ritorno a Firenze, ho viaggato subito en treno per Roma. Quando sono arrivato a Roma, sono stato ricevuto da una delegazione papale che mi ha detto che Il Papa mi stava aspettando ansiosamente. Siccome io e Il Papa siamo buoni amici da molti anni, io sono stato portato subito alla Cittá del Vaticano in una macchina speciale accompagnato da molti motoscuteri con guardie Papali e sirene.

Il Papa mi stava aspettando nel bar Papale e voleva comprare una bibita da una macchina distributrice per me. Sfortunatamente, la veste papale non ha tasche. Il Papa non aveva soldi, e per questo io ho comprato la bibita per noi due.

Felici di essere riuniti dopo molti anni, Il Papa ed io abbiamo chiacchierato per due ore di baseball, calcio, donne, e altri argomenti che qui non posso rivelare. Il Papa si è confessato con me. È stato molto interessante, ma qui non posso rivelare i dettagli sensazionali.

Dopo la chiacchierata, Il Papa mi ha portato alla Cappella Sistina, dove lui ha organizzato una festa con musica (di tipo) "salsa". Noi abbiamo trovato lì molti preti, molte giovani monache, e alcune donne attraenti. Noi ci siamo divertiti molto, ma qui non posso rivelare tutti i dettagli sensazionali.

HAY CERVEZA?

Hay cerveza?

Si, hay,
Pero no tenemos.

IN DEFENSE OF MEDIOCRITY

Letters to the Editor, and Others, on the Controversy

Letters by
  EDWARD A. TOMLINSON
  Associate Professor, Univeristy of Maryland Law School
  Signed by 12 other members of the law school faculty
  JOSEPH KRAFT
  Washington
  J. LAWRENCE SCHULTZ
  Editor, *Harvard Law Review*, Cambridge, Masschusetts
  The letter was co-signed by 57 of the 70 active *Harvard Law Review* members

The defense of Judge G. Harrold Carswell's mediocrity by Senators Hruska and Long on the basis that mediocrity should be represented on the Supreme Court is the most incredible reason I have ever heard for appointment of a man to one of the most important and responsible positions in our society. This is truly a perversion of the idea of democracy, aside from the racist view that Carswell also represents. In any case, the standard of mediocrity has already been heavily represented in President Nixon's prior appointments, and it is clearly over-represented in Congress.

It appears to me that the crisis in our nation is so great that it is time for us to strive to seek out the best among us for these awesome responsibilities, rather than reaching for the lowest common denominator.

The appointment of Judge Carswell and the defense of mediocrity are insults to the intelligence and patience of the American people.

  —Warren M. Hern, M.D.
    Washington, D.C.

FLYING WITH GERALDO

WHEN I FIRST ARRIVED in northeast Brazil as a Peace Corps physician in August, 1966, my first duty post was Recife, the capitol of the state of Pernambuco. Recife ("reef," in English) sits at the point of Brazil that juts out into the Atlantic closest to Africa. In fact, this piece of real estate used to be tucked up into that corner of Africa where the coast bends south toward the Congo and Angola—about 200 million years ago.

Northeast Brazil is mostly a dry, hardscrabble place where men dig for water with their bare hands, where sugar cane plantations once dominated the economy, and where life is hard. One of my first trips was into the interior of the state of Paraiba, just north of Pernambuco, where I traveled along the dusty roads to tiny villages visiting isolated volunteers with the local Peace Corps representative, Roy Tucker. We visited a legendary Irish priest who lived the most admirable and enduring Christian values of loving dedication to his flock and humble hard work. He inspired thousands. The Peace Corps volunteers admired him, worked with him, and joined his efforts.

When I got back to Recife after this first shake-down outing, I was told I must fly to Salvador, Bahia, immediately to evacuate a Peace Corps volunteer who had been injured and who was temporarily under care at a hospital deep in the interior of Bahia. I was told I would be met at the airport by a local pilot, Geraldo, who would fly me in a light plane to the volunteer where we could pick him up.

As soon as the large prop-jet plane carrying me from Recife landed, I was met by Geraldo, a young Brazilian who, I was told, was an expert at navigating the enormous distances of the interior—sort of a Latin American bush pilot.

Geraldo and I hit it off immediately. He was typically Brazilian in his warmth, friendliness, and loquaciousness. He was confident, and I thought the whole adventure was great fun. I loved to fly in small planes, and I would get to see the geography of the interior much better at low altitude.

Awhile after we took off, Geraldo asked me if I had ever piloted a plane. I said I had—a couple of times—but only in flight and not landing or takeoff. He showed me how to control the plane, showed me the compass bearing, and watched me fly for awhile. I loved it. But I was glad I didn't have to try to land.

It was a beautiful, sunny day and easy to see the landmarks. After about an hour, we saw a fair-sized town up ahead and Geraldo started a descent. We circled the dirt strip, and Geraldo buzzed it a few times to scare the cows and burros off it so we could land. The last low pass over Greater Metropolitan Vittoria da Conquista was also a way to get somebody from town to drive out in a Jeep to pick us up.

Sure enough, a few minutes after we landed and got out of the plane, a battered Jeep that may have survived the Normandy Invasion came bouncing across the field toward us.

We piled in and headed for the local Catholic hospital (actually, the only kind of hospital out there). Geraldo headed off to get gas for the plane. I walked into the hospital, was greeted by a friendly nun, and asked to see the Peace Corps volunteer, Tom McCarthy, who was under care there for a broken pelvis. McCarthy, a Boston taxi driver before becoming a Peace Corps volunteer, had sustained grievous injuries, including a broken pelvis, when the Peace Corps Jeep he was riding in with a colleague had missed a turn on a country road and rolled over.

The nun looked at me and said sweetly, *"Está na rua."* (He's out on the street.) *"Esta na rua?"* I asked incredulously. *"Como é—éle é muito ferido e não deve caminar!"* (How is that? He's seriously injured and shouldn't be walking!) The nun shook her head and pointed to the street.

Alarmed, confused, and apprehensive about both my "patient" and the conflict between what I thought I knew about him and what the nun was telling me, I hurried out to the front of the hospital and looked frantically for the fugitive Peace Corps volunteer/Boston taxicab driver/self-styled rebel whose insouciance and incorrigible defiance of the rules was legendary among his fellow volunteers.

There he was, hunching down the sidewalk by putting his support on two little "crutches" that only came up to his hips, then swinging his legs forward to take a step. It had to be McCarthy.

I walked up to him, appalled that he was out like this, but admiring his tenacity, anyway—but to do what? "Hey, are you Tom McCarthy?" I yelled to him from behind. "Yeah, who are you?" he replied in his most contemptuous Boston cabdriver wise-crack Irish voice. "I'm Doctor Hern. I'm the new Peace Corps doctor." "Oh, yeah? Where'd ya go ta medical school?" "The University of Colorado." "Izzat accredited?" he fired back. "Don't give me any shit. Where do you think you're going?" "I'm goin' ta get some cigarettes, shit-head." "You get your ass back in the hospital right now. You can get your cigarettes later. I'm taking you back to Salvador." "Go fuck yerself." "Either you turn around or I'll pick you up and carry you back, asshole. Don't be an idiot. Don't you want to be outta this shithole?" "It's no shithole, fuckface."

Sensing rebellion and lack of cooperation, I walked in front of McCarthy and turned to stand in front of him. He was a skinny little Irish kid with freckles all over his pale skin. He couldn't weigh over a hundred pounds. He was wiry. I liked him. I thought the whole thing was a scream, but I didn't want to let him know I thought it was hilarious. I knew I could pick him up if I had to. He looked up at me, stopped, and turned around. He started hunching back to the hospital.

"Look, Tom, you have a broken pelvis. You could hurt yourself for life. I'm gonna take you where you can really get over this." "Ah, shuddup," he explained (my respects to Damon Runyon).

After a short interval while McCarthy gathered up his belongings in a little bundle and I thanked the nuns for their care for this sweet, adorable patient, we made our way out to the Jeep driven by Geraldo. There was no wheelchair, so Tom hunched his way out to that destination.

We piled into the Cessna 180 that was now refueled from the barrels behind the back passenger seat. Tom sat in the back. I sat in the co-pilot's seat. Some kids scared the cows off the dirt runway, and we took off. It was a beautiful day with unlimited visibility.

After about an hour of flying, clouds appeared, and the visibility started getting less. The clouds got lower and lower, and Geraldo kept going lower and lower. Then I noticed that once in awhile he would lift up his sunglasses and squint in different directions. "What are you looking for?" I asked him. "*Estou buscando um buraco,*" he replied ("I'm looking for a hole in the clouds"). "Why are you taking off your glasses?" I asked. "Because they're too dark to see the holes, but they're made for my eyes." "Look, Geraldo, you fly the plane, and I'll look for the *buracos,*" I said. Meanwhile, the rain was now hitting the windshield and it was getting darker. It was only about a half-hour until sunset.

Geraldo had a fourteen-year-old girlfriend in Valencia, just across the bay from Salvador, and he planned to stop there to see her. This was an excellent idea since we were almost out of gas, the clouds were getting lower by the minute, it was raining, and it would be dark in a few minutes. Geraldo set the plane down in a flawless landing on a dirt strip that ended at the edge of the Bay of All Saints, on the other side of which we could see the city of Salvador. The Baianos irreverently call this remarkable town "Saint Savior of The Bay of Almost All Saints *(São Salvador da Bahia de Quasi Todos Os Santos)* because, frankly, it is not a very saintly place, even with a church for every day of the year.

Tom and I each had a cell in a little hotel by the "airport," Geraldo got laid, and we took off for Salvador the next morning. About a month later, I evacuated Tom to Gorgas Hospital in the Canal Zone where I had done my internship. My ambulance driver buddies met us at the airport. As far as I know, Tom McCarthy went back to driving cabs in Boston.

On our later flights into the interior of Bahia to visit Peace Corps volunteers and check up on their health, Geraldo would show me the compass bearing, crawl into the back seat, and go to sleep. I would know he was awake when I smelled cigarette smoke along with the gas fumes. As I think about it now, I can't believe the plane didn't blow up somewhere over Bahia. Geraldo was a good pilot, but he was a little crazy. So, it could be argued, was I. It is amazing that I am still alive.

115

UMA ZONA BEM GRANDE

WHEN I ACCEPTED AN ASSIGNMENT as a Peace Corps physician in Brazil, I was still doing my internship at Gorgas Hospital in the Canal Zone. My 1963 Volkswagen Beetle had accompanied me to Panama on a ship from New Orleans, so I had the use of it there. So I got to spend some weekends dancing and socializing at the fiestas in small towns on the Azuero Peninsula, swimming and enjoying the beaches with some local Peace Corps volunteers, and taking Spanish lessons in downtown Panama City. One of my best friends in the Spanish class was a Maryknoll nun from Hawaii. I think her name was Maira.

Guarare and Las Tablas were little towns especially famous for their Saturday all-night dance parties accompanied by spectacularly good musical groups. The Columbian beat was better than any drug one could possibly imagine. You could not be conscious and aware of the rhythm without wanting to dance. We would dance until dawn, have breakfast, then drive back to take call at the hospital. Our chiefs didn't know the difference, and the patients survived.

When the time came to leave Panama for my Brazilian assignment, the Peace Corps said they would ship my car to Rio de Janeiro. This was a long way from my duty post in Salvador, Bahia, but it didn't matter. It would be a good adventure to drive it up to Bahia, about 1,000 miles.

It is still my belief that the Peace Corps shipped my car by way of the Suez Canal. It took about a year for the car to get to Rio. Not to worry, I had frequent trips to Rio on Peace Corps business, and I had made the acquaintance of a charming and intellectually stimulating young Brazilian woman there. I always looked forward to our endless conversations about philosophy, traffic flow patterns in Rio de Janeiro, and Brazilian agricultural economics.

Upon starting my drive back up to Bahia, I found when I stopped for gas or refreshments that there was extraordinary attention given to the Volkswagen. It seems that there was a Volkswagen factory in southern Brazil (São Paulo, I think), and the Brazilians were keenly interested in comparing the Brazilian models with one that looked, well, different somehow. They knew it was probably made in Germany, but they always asked. Every single person asked me where the car was made. They would make admiring sounds, touch the car, open and close the doors, look inside, and ask to see the motor. They would invariably say that the German-made Volkswagen was highly superior to the same cars made in Brazil. It was an irresistable subject for conversation among the Brazilians. My license plate, which read "Canal Zone," seemed to be a matter of particular fascination.

It did not occur to me once, in noticing this interest in the license plate, that the word "zone" in most of Latin America refers to a neighborhood of whorehouses, a red-light district.

As I passed through the state of Minas Gerais, about half-way to my destination, I stopped by the way at a little shop and station to get gas and to buy some of the wonderful *queijo minas* cheese, a treat not to be missed. This was accompanied by a few crackers and a *cafezinho*, a demitasse of Brazilian coffee strong enough to require two hands for stirring.

After paying for the gas and having my refreshment, I came out to find several Brazilian *camponeses* (peasants) standing around my car and admiring it from a short distance, talking among themselves. As I approached, they greeted me courteously and in a friendly way, as was customary, and I returned the greetings: *"Boa tarde, o senhor, como vai?"* (Good afternoon, Mister, how are you?) *"Muito bem, obrigado, e voce?"* (Just fine, thanks, and you?). We all shook hands, as was customary. I waited politely for my new friends to satiate themselves with their inspection of my car.

At this point, one wiry, weather-beaten field hand with a disintegrating straw hat pulled me aside behind the car and, pointing at the license plate, asked me (very politely), *"O senhor, de onde e esta placa?"* (Mister, where is this license plate from?) *"Da Zona de Canal em Panama,"* I replied ("From the Panama Canal Zone"). *"Da Zona de Canal?"* he remarked in wonder, shaking his head. He thought for a moment, looking at the license plate, trying to take it all in.

Finally, he spoke, quietly, in almost reverential tones: *"Deve ser uma zona bem grande implacar carros tambem!"* (Must be a helluva big zone that they can license cars, too!).

THE SURGERY LESSONS

On the porch of the house I had rented with my medical school classmates, I relaxed in my hammock, enjoying the beautiful Colorado spring day. The hammock was a souvenir from my 1962 experience in eastern Nicaragua working as a "camp doctor" in a mining camp. It was woven of tree-bark twine by the Miskito Indians of the savannah. I was also contemplating my uncertain fate.

About a year before, in the spring of 1963, I had written a letter to Dr. Theodor Binder, a German physician who had founded a hospital in the Peruvian Amazon to provide medical care for the Indian people in the area. Dr. Binder had been a protégé of Albert Schweitzer, my hero and inspiration to study medicine, and he had established his hospital in his mentor's tradition. The hospital was called the "Hospital Amazonico 'Albert Schweitzer'," and I had learned about it through the Unitarian Service Committee. I thought it would be a good experience to work in Dr. Binder's hospital. Instead of being in the protective cocoon of the university hospital, where I had been invited to spend the summer between medical school terms doing laboratory work in a whitewashed windowless cubicle, thereby proving my dedication to the Medical Establishment, it seemed to me that working in that hospital would be a way of really finding out about the human condition and doing something directly about human suffering. I was not yet a physician, but this was what I wanted to know about.

I also wanted to understand something about native cultures. I had minored in anthropology as an undergraduate and saw the intersection of public health and anthropology as fascinating. I wanted to understand how people in other cultures looked at health and disease, at healing, and how their view of the world affected their concepts about these things. Although these questions formed the basis of the new discipline of "medical anthropology," I didn't know that and didn't know it was being invented.

I also wanted to learn about tropical medicine. In my readings about Albert Schweitzer and other missionary doctors, and in my classes on pathology and microbiology, I was fascinated by the tropical diseases that were so different from the routine diseases affecting most Americans.

Since I had no money, I had searched the foundation directories and had found that the Wenner-Gren Foundation for Anthropological Research seemed to be interested in these subjects. I wrote the director a letter requesting $1,000 (their limit) to go to Peru to work for awhile at Binder's hospital and then to do research among the native people there in health issues. It turns out that the director, Paul Fejos, a physician and anthropologist who had conducted important research among the Peruvian Amazon tribes, had just died, although I did not know this. His widow, Lita Fejos, was the person who answered my letters. Later, I learned that she saw me continuing in her late husband's tradition.

It was now one week after the winter quarter had ended, and I had no idea what would happen next. Dr. Binder had invited me to come to work in his 28-bed hospital where he had workers from about five different countries who spoke among them about ten languages. I spoke a little Spanish from my self-taught experience in Nicaragua. The mining camp workers had taught me one word at a time and found my mistakes hilarious. I was the cheapest entertainment in camp.

The phone rang. It was somebody from the Wenner-Gren Foundation. They were sending me a check for $1,000. I paid some bills, bought a portable typewriter and a cheap camera, and bought a plane ticket to Lima. I could only afford to buy a ticket back to Miami, and that left me with $200 that would have to last me for six months. I would get my room and board while working at Dr. Binder's hospital.

Lima was fascinating. I learned to save money by buying *anticuchos y choclos* (beef-heart chunks on a splinter and fresh roasted corn) from old ladies selling food from sidewalk stands around the Plaza San Martin. I would always cook the anticuchos over the grill a little longer to kill the beef heartworm that might be in the meat, then soak them in *salsa de aji*, which I calculated would kill anything else.

The Peace Corps physicians in Lima took me under their wings and gave me encouragement. Tom Hakala was a surgeon who had worked at Dr. Binder's hospital, and that was a new inspiration.

We didn't fly over the Andes in the unpressurized c-46; we flew between them. And I found that my residence at high altitude in Colorado didn't keep me from needing oxygen from the face mask.

We came down through the clouds over the Amazon rain forest and saw an endless carpet of green foliage laced with tiny light brown streams. After a bumpy landing at what passed for the Pucallpa Airport, I found myself trying to figure out how to get to the Hospital Amazonico. I must have looked disoriented, because some missionaries from the Summer Institute of Linguistics offered me a ride in the back of their jeep. They dropped me off just outside the gate of the hospital.

I was escorted into the laboratory, the only air-conditioned room in the hospital, which was staffed by a beautiful young woman, Pam Wagner. Pretty soon, Dr. Binder appeared wearing slacks, a long sport shirt, and sandals. His eyebrows were immense and gave him a surprised appearance. My first impression was that he was a kind of holy man. He spoke to me in a soft voice, his precise English accented by German.

Dr. Binder's passion was mycology, and he was about to go to a conference in Europe to present his research and raise money for the hospital. In the 28-bed hospital, there were about forty patients, many of them in beds in the hallways. Dr. Binder's interest in mycology sprang from the fact that many of the patients had systemic fungal diseases, most unknown in the United States outside medical textbooks. Other patients had the full range of tropical diseases from leishmaniasis in various forms to tropical ulcer to pemphigus vulgaris to leprosy and malaria. The tuberculosis patients were in a separate structure.

Every afternoon, there was an outpatient ambulatory clinic, and I was put in charge of seeing those patients. Using my University of Chicago paperback Spanish dictionary, it would sometimes take me a half-hour to see a patient since I declined to have a translator. I made exceptions for Indians who didn't speak Spanish. It soon became clear that most of the health problems of the people I was seeing (primarily Mestizo, not Native American) were the result of major public health and economic problems. Individual treatment was helpful and gratifying but no solution.

About a week after I arrived, I learned two things: first, Dr. Binder's temporary replacement would be Dr. Michael Diana, a surgeon from New York City who spoke English and Italian but no Spanish; second, none of the patients in the hospital had been "worked up," that is, had a history and complete physical examination as well as laboratory work. These were essential, in my training, for an accurate diagnosis and rational treatment plan. I set out to do a "work up" on each patient in the hospital.

My first impression of Dr. Diana was of a man who was used to being in charge. He had piercing black eyes and a gruff but friendly manner. He had total self-confidence and carried himself that way. A few short black hairs grew out of the ridge of his Italian nose. A man of about sixty, he moved with a positive and athletic step. He was direct. No bullshit.

Dr. Diana and I hit it off. We liked each other. He had worked at other outposts in Africa and Haiti, and he liked what I was doing. But he took one look at the operating room, which was being used for storage, and said, "I'm going home." "I'm a professional. I can't work here. I have standards." There were no trained operating room personnel. The quiet, slender Peruvian "nurse," Rosa Torres, had no formal training as a nurse. The German nurse, who really *was* a nurse, was a survivor of Allied bombing during the Second World War that had killed her entire family, and she hated all Americans.

I said, "Give me two weeks to see what I can do." We cleaned out the operating room and scrubbed it down. I turned an empty (but clean) garbage

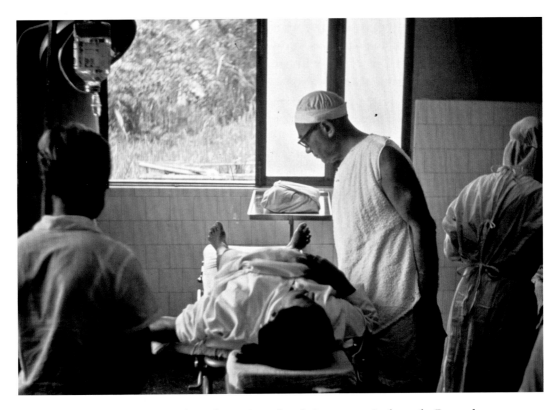

can into a water storage tank with a spigot for doing a surgical scrub. I got the laundry ladies to make us some scrub clothes, including sleeveless terrycloth shirts for Dr. Diana and me. I taught Rosa, Pam, and Crystal how to be a scrub nurse, OR assistant, and circulating nurse, respectively. Dottie Satterfield, a Peace Corps volunteer who worked at the hospital as an x-ray technician, sat in to see what she could do. I gave them classes on sterile technique and instrument handling. We made surgical drapes and prep sheets. We learned how to make bandages and dress wounds. In two weeks, we started operating.

In the meantime, Dr. Diana and I developed a friendship and camaraderie as I sought out his advice on diagnostic issues and various other matters. After lunch in the hospital mess, we would put on our bathing trunks and walk down through the meadow to the lake, borrow a canoe from one of the Shipibo Indian families camped on the lakeshore, and go out to loaf in the sun and swim. The water was warm and addictive. We would talk about all kinds of subjects including the fact that I had discovered that the cockroaches were eating all the carbon paper that we used for making copies of the x-ray reports.

"Someday, Warren," Dr. Diana said to me as I swam around the canoe one day, "you'll be gone and I'll be gone, and the cockroaches will take over the hospital."

121 ✳

One of my most vivid memories is of Dr. Diana in his white boxer trunks, terrycloth t-shirt, and white cotton surgery cap made by the laundry ladies, stalking the operating room in his slipper socks with a flyswatter, killing all the flies in the operating room before we prepped the patient.

Our first case was a hernia repair on a poor man whose scrotum, filled with small bowel, hung down an extra five or six inches. He had a double hernia. It was the first case I would do as the primary surgeon since my surgery rotation as a third-year medical student. But first, I had had to figure out a way to do anesthesia. Dr. Diana said he didn't know anything about anesthesia.

Out in the storage building behind the hospital, I found some vials of dried Pontocaine. The instructions were to do a spinal tap, draw off 10cc of spinal fluid, break the top off the vial, squirt the spinal fluid into the vial, mix it up with the dried Pontocaine, draw this mixture back up into the syringe, and then inject it back into the patient's spinal canal. Yikes!

So I did. And it worked. During my three-month surgical rotation, I had learned how to do spinal anesthesia. I was the one-eyed man in the land of the blind, the other inhabitant being Dr. Diana, who, as a professor of surgical anatomy at the New York Medical School at Flower and Fifth Avenue, had never given a spinal anesthesia. He had done abdominal surgery on gored cowboys from rodeos at Madison Square Garden, he had saved gunshot Mafia dons, but I was ahead of him on this one.

We did fourteen cases under my primitive spinal anesthesia including a hysterectomy on a Shipibo woman in whom I had made a diagnosis of cervical cancer. One woman had a uterine fibroid tumor the size of a grapefruit hanging from her vagina.

Each day I would get up at 6:00 A.M., make rounds, make chart notes on each patient, and get the new operating room crew ready for the day's case. After breakfast with Dr. Diana and the hospital staff, we would go to the operating room and "hew flesh," as the surgeons say. All the cases went extremely well, although I knew the prognosis for the Shipibo woman with cervical cancer was grim. We would have lunch with lots of lemonade. Dr. Diana and I would go to the lake. In the afternoon, I would see about thirty to forty patients in the clinic. We would have dinner with lots of lemonade. Then I would take a shower, my third of the day. Then I would go to Dr. Diana's room, where we would have a surgery lesson.

First, Dr. Diana would ask me to recite for him the anatomy of the case we were to do the next day. I would then describe each step of the operation beginning with what kind of an incision I would make, how big, at what angle, etc. I would have to tell him what layers of tissue I would encounter, the names of the blood vessels, the names and branches of each nerve in the region, and the

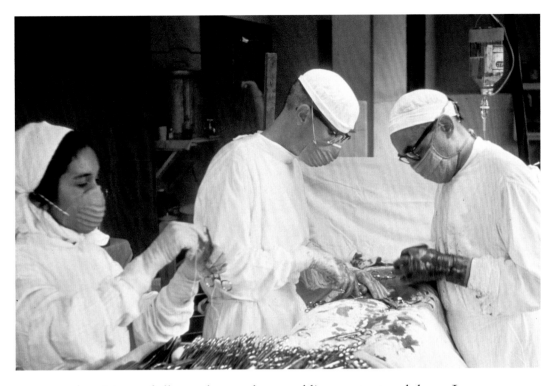

names and positions of all muscles, tendons, and ligaments at each layer. I would describe for him which instruments I would use for each step, what I would ask my assistant (him) to do at each step, how I would explore the incision site and identify the pathology, what I would do to correct it, what layers I would suture on the way back out, what kind of suture material I would use for each layer, what kind of stitch I would use and how I would make it—with which hand and with what instrument, and how I would close the skin. I would then recite what postoperative care I would give including fluid management, wound care, and recuperation instructions.

Dr. Diana would tell me his philosophy of surgery, which emphasized good surgical technique, a precise knowledge of surgical anatomy, antisepsis, wound debridement, and good postoperative care. We talked about Ambroise Paré, a French physician who laid down these principles in the seventeenth century.

After that, Dr. Diana would give me a glass of cheap gin, no ice or mix, and we would talk about politics, history, women, the Mob, his childhood friends in Italian Harlem, most of whom were now dead or in Sing Sing, and what he would say in Italian to a Mafioso who wouldn't pay his bill. Even though I didn't speak Italian, I could understand that it had something to do with the man's hide being tacked to the wall and something about a dead cat. It was pretty clear that Dr. Diana was not a man whose instructions could be taken lightly.

The fifteenth case was a Shipibo woman, Virginia, from a village high up the Calleria River, a remote place near the border of Brazil. She had been in the hospital for months without a diagnosis and was receiving many kinds of medicine. Through a Shipibo interpreter, I learned that she had had a baby a year before, the child who shared her bed in the hospital. When she had her baby, the village midwife had told her that she had twins, but one of the twins did not come out.

Virginia had had a fever for a long time, but she didn't have a cough and didn't seem to have tuberculosis. She did have a mass that extended from under her rib cage on the left side down into her pelvis, across the midline, and was about the size of a very large football. Examining her, I found a strange tube descending across the top of this mass, and the tube had bowel sounds. On x-ray, it looked like bowel, probably the colon. This meant that the mass was retroperitoneal, and since it was on one side, it was probably her left kidney, and since she had a fever and white cells in her urine, it probably meant that she had a pyonephrosis—a kidney full of pus. The left side of the pelvic bone was much smaller than the right side, meaning this problem had been there for a very long time.

There was no way we could do this under spinal anesthesia. It was too dangerous and complicated. But there was no one in the hospital who knew how to give general anesthesia. So I taught Crystal and Carmen (Dr. Binder's wife) how to give open-drop ether anesthesia.

Two Peace Corps volunteers associated with the hospital, John and Dottie Satterfield, had built a house down by the Shipibo camp. In addition to being the hospital's x-ray technician, Dottie also taught the Shipibo women how to use a sewing machine, and John was a carpenter. John fixed up a vacuum pump with the little motor outside the hospital so it would not cause an explosion with the ether. About twenty feet of tubing allowed us to have a vacuum for wound suction.

As soon as Dr. Diana opened a flank incision in our patient, her blood pressure dropped to zero even though she had a pulse. The blood in the operating field was dark. Lighten up the anesthesia. Stick-tie and cut. Stick-tie and cut. Grab that bleeder. Put your hand behind the kidney. Cut the ureter. Clamp the artery. Cut. Tie. Where's the edge of the peritoneum? Gimme that clamp. *Tijeras* (scissors). *Hilo* (thread). What's her pulse? Gimme a 2-o silk. Skin. Close. Run the stitch. Lock.

The operation took about an hour. The patient's kidney contained four liters of pus. She came out of the anesthesia after awhile and threw up. We did input and output on her fluids; nobody had ever heard of it before. A week later, she went back to her village with clear urine. Thirty years later, Virginia still lived in Calleria.

In June, Dr. Diana got on a DC-3 in Pucallpa and flew in between the Andes back to Lima and then back to New York. I went to Paococha, a Shipibo village, to do research. Rosa, the woman on whom we had done the hysterectomy for advanced cervical cancer, was my neighbor in Paococha. I lived next door in her daughter's house, which I shared in her family's absence with Frank Billman, a Peace Corps volunteer.

Rosa played with her grandchildren. She smiled at me. She cooked in her kitchen, a campfire under a thatch roof on the bank of the lake, and brought me food. Her husband, Pablo, was a wonderful man with a calm and cheerful disposition, and we became warm friends. Rosa died later that year.

When I came back five years later, in 1969, to do research in Paococha for six weeks, Pablo was there, living with his daughters' families. He would sit in my hammock, talking quietly and laughing now and then as we discussed things that were happening in the village. He was a splendid woodcarver and artisan. His canoe paddles, which he carved while surrounded by his grandchildren, were perfect works of art.

Five years later, when I was back again to do research, my dear friend Pablo was wasting away from tuberculosis. He died later that year.

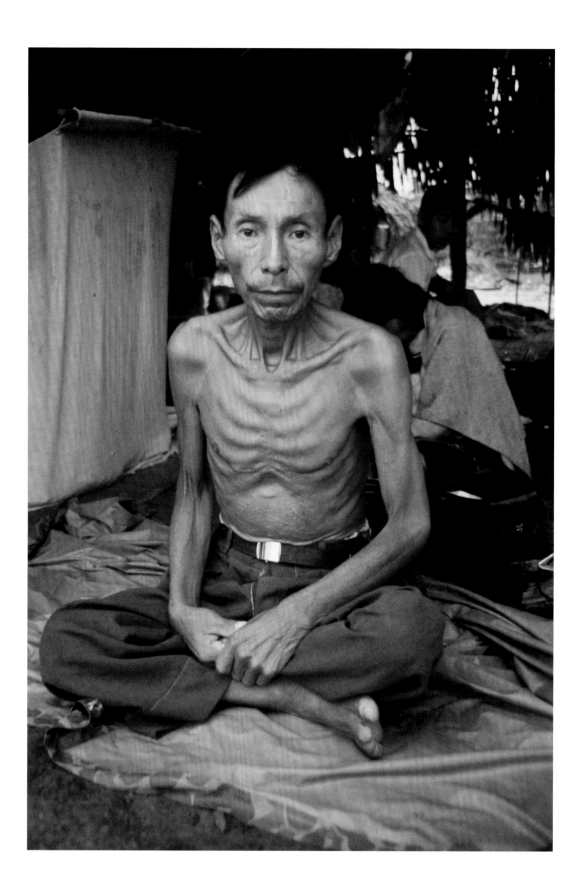

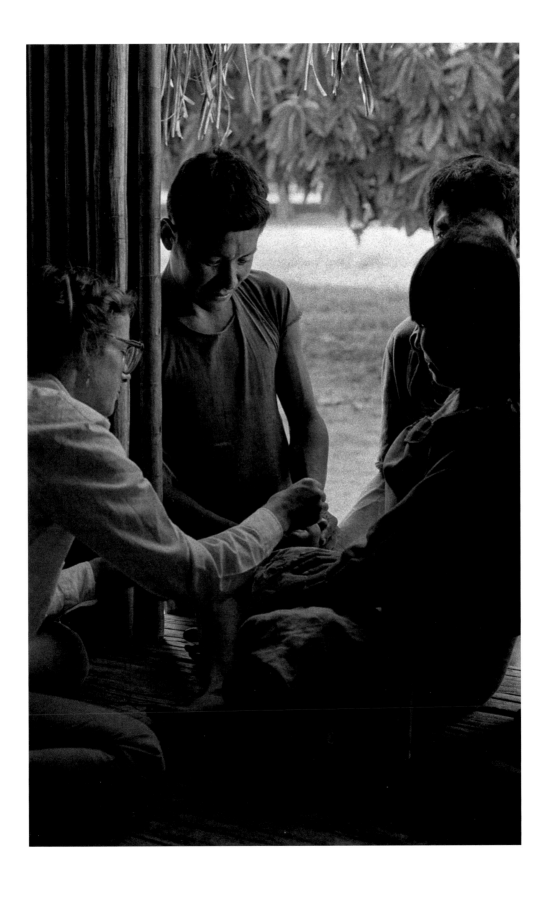

KEEP YOUR WORMS WARM

On the 21st of May, 1955, my dad and I got up early because it was the opening day of the Colorado fishing season, always a big day for us. But surprise!—the snow was two feet deep in the back yard. It was probably deeper in the high mountains where we were going to fish. But we put our gear in the truck and left, anyway.

After a long drive, we got to Buffalo Creek and got our fishing gear assembled. Since there was a good stream that was not too deep or rocky for solid footing, we walked along the bank and found a place where we could wade out and cast spinners into the riffles just below the big rocks. Trout hung out in the quiet places behind the rocks, and the turbulence of the water in those places got the spinners going. Besides, it was too cold for worms.

We fished for several hours and my dad only caught one fish. I didn't catch any. But after awhile, we noticed this guy on the other side of the crick who was catching a fish every fifteen or twenty minutes. We couldn't stand it. What was he doing?

Finally, my dad hollered out to him, "What are they hittin' on—flies?" No answer. The guy ignored us. My dad was getting frustrated, especially when he caught his hook on a rock and couldn't get it loose right away.

Trying again, my dad hollered, "What's yer luck? What'er you usin'?" No answer. An hour passed. The guy kept hauling in fish. It was getting late. My dad hollered again, "Hey, buddy, yer doin' great. What's yer secret?"

With this, the guy finally put down his fishing rod, cupped both hands in front of his mouth, and spit out a blob of something. "You gotta keep yer worms warm," he said. "But ya gotta keep 'em in the front a yer mouth so they don't get loose."

REPORT ON
THE EPIDEMIC OF CHOLERA

Report on the Epidemic of Cholera
On the
Pisqui River and Lower Ucayali, Peru
Trip of 8 June to 20 June, 1991
made by
Warren M. Hern, M.D., M.P.H., Ph.D.
Epidemiologist
University of Colorado
and
University of Colorado Health Sciences Center
Boulder and Denver, Colorado, U.S.A.

Report prepared for
Special program of the Campaign Against Cholera
Regional Health Center
Pucallpa, Peru
21 June 1991

_____(signed)_____
Warren M. Hern, M.D., M.P.H., Ph.D.
Translated from original Spanish version

ON JUNE 8, 1991, I left Yarinachocha in a motorized canoe of 11.5 meters with a crew of four Shipibo men bound for Paoyhän and the lower Pisqui River, where I had been conducting public health studies for several years. My first visit to Paococha/Paoyhän was in 1964, when I was a third year medical student a the University of Colorado School of Medicine, and I made subsequent visits in 1969, 1974, 1979, 1983–84, 1985, 1989, and, in 1990, to Paoyhän and nine communities on the Pisqui. During these trips, among other things, I conducted a smallpox vaccination campaign during the smallpox epidemic of 1964, training three Shipibo men to help me, one of whom, Eleodoro Maynas C., continues as the head of my crew. I also conducted studies in this area leading to my Master of Public Health degree and Ph.D. in Epidemiology at the University of North Carolina School of Public Health.

On this trip, I took a quantity of materials and medicines against cholera given to me by the Regional Health Center of Pucallpa. The quantity of treatments were sufficient for ten persons who were gravely ill and sufficient for a small number of persons less sick. I also had a small quantity of medicine and materials that I bought in Peru, and I also brought medicine from my own medical office in the United States. These included doses sufficient to treat a small number of people for tuberculosis (given by Merrel Lepetit DOW of Latin America), and medicines for gastrointestinal parasites, anemia, dermatitis, wounds, bronchitis, infections, and conjunctivitis.

Arriving in Paoyhän, I found that there had been various cases of cholera and that people were either recuperating or under treatment by the practical nurse sent by the Contamana Regional Health Center. One patient, Lola I., was gravely ill but recuperating thanks to the treatment given by the nurse. She had just finished receiving intravenous treatment for dehydration from cholera. The treatment given by the nurse, with tetracycline and rehydration by intravenous and oral routes, was exactly correct. The patient's mother was with her in the mosquito net, in the custom of the Shipibo, to assist with treatment and to give the oral rehydration solution. Her father also was there to help. Both parents developed symptoms of cholera about a week later. On Tuesday, 18 June, Lola was recuperating well but appeared much better with good hydration and an absence of most symptoms of cholera. She just felt tired and weak.

As far as I could determine, there were no deaths due to cholera in Paoyhän (population about 1,000). I do not know how many cases of cholera occurred.

Since the nurse had used up most of her materials, I gave her materials sufficient to treat five persons gravely ill with cholera.

On 9 June, with my regular crew of three Shipibo men, including Eleodoro Maynas, Tomás Ramirez Cairuna, and Humberto Rojas Martinez, and also Sr. Marcial Rodriquez, laboratory technician, I embarked for Contamana to advise the military command that we were going to go up the Pisqui River. Arriving at 6:00 P.M., still in daylight, we were surrounded by soldiers armed with machine guns pointed at us. The soldiers demanded our documents and interrogated us one-by-one for an hour. They kept the documents of my Shipibo colleagues. One, the chief of my crew, with whom I have worked for twenty-seven years, was interrogated intensively for a long time because his voting registration booklet contained a small erasure and correction made by the registrar who prepared it. A soldier with a machine gun was ordered to go through all my bags of medicine, clothes, food, tools, mosquito net, and toilet paper. Now that it was dark, the soldier took one of my flashlights with two batteries that was for the use of my crew. Later, he showed me the flashlight and said that he was going to keep it. I insisted that he return the flashlight but he would not listen to me until I said I would speak to the commander about the problem. We continued with this intensive discussion for fifteen minutes, during which his machine gun swung carelessly from his shoulder, until he finally gave me back the flashlight.

The commander, a gentleman who treated me with respect, told me that I was running a grave risk to go up the Pisqui because of the terrorism and subversion there, but I replied that I was not afraid because the Shipibo people are my friends; they know me to the point of having adopted me as a son of the Shipibo, and that I had worked there since 1983. Furthermore, although there might be criminal extortion on the Pisqui as there is in other parts of the world, there is no political movement there that I know of. The people have more danger of dying from cholera, tuberculosis, or accidental shots from the soldiers than they do from terrorism. That is my opinion. The commander ended the conversation with a recommendation that I stay in the Hotel Florencia of Contamana near the waterfront.

Just the same, we were ordered to appear at the command headquarters at 8:00 A.M. the next morning, and we arrived at 8:00 A.M. Again, we were surrounded by soldiers with machine guns as they came out of their sandbag bunkers. From there, we were escorted by the commander with his machine gun and other heavily armed soldiers to my boat, watching out to avoid being hit or otherwise attacked by children playing football or women carrying water. A different soldier armed with a machine gun was again ordered to go through my bags, and I was interrogated by him about the purpose of my trip to the Pisqui and the dosage of medicines for tuberculosis and cholera. After one-and-a-half hours of interrogation, we were released to go. We left Contamana going upriver at 9:30 A.M.

That day, June 10, we traveled up the Ucayali from Contamana, arriving at about 5:00 P.M. at a Shipibo camp on the beach across from the mouth of the Pisqui River. This camp of one family, that pertained now to the village of Santa Maria, was devastated by cholera. I knew some of those who had died and some of the survivors when they lived in other villages on the Pisqui. The dead included:

Aurelio Mejia Ubillos	27 years	d. 15 May 1991
Luzmila Macedo Acho	60 years	d. 20 May 1991
Rosa Inuma Macedo	45 years	d. 21 May 1991

Luzmila, the mother of Rosa and mother-in-law of Aurelio, became ill at about 5:00 P.M. and died at midnight. Rosa died in Tumbes, where she was receiving treatment from the health department nurse.

We camped on the beach right by the mouth of the Pisqui, leaving at 6:15 A.M. to go up the river. At 7:30, we found a camp of Shipibo from various communities. One, Alfonso Saldaña, whom I knew from the Pisqui community of Tupac Amaru, was weak from cholera but, according to his companions, recuperating. Alfonso was taking oral hydration solution. I felt his state of hydration was acceptable and that he could take oral medication and oral solutioin. I gave him tetracycline 250 mg. q.i.d. for seven days and left a quantity of the packets of oral rehydration salts, and I instructed his friends on the preparation. We continued our journey. Within three days, we heard that Alfonso had died the day after I saw him (11 June) and gave him his treatment. We confirmed his death on 17 June.

We stopped at the community of Ninth of October for two hours to collect the data necessary for my study of public health of the Shipibo of the Pisqui. We did not find anyone ill with cholera and no history of deaths. We continued and arrived at Santa Rosa at 5:30 P.M. During the next day, I conducted my study in Santa Rosa until 3:00 P.M. without encountering any cases of cholera in the communty. At 4:00 P.M., we arrived in Irazola.

In Irazola, we were received by Alcibiades Valera, the health promoter,[1] with whom I had worked previously. We were given lodging next to a house that had been burned because its owner had died from cholera. It is a custom of the Shipibo to burn the house of an adult who has died. This father of a family of several children, Armando Morey, was forty years old. He died on 18 May after being sick for twelve hours.

There were two other cases of cholera in the community, one of whom, Laura T., had been sick for five days. Laura had received treatment at the medical post in Frey Martin and had been discharged. She continued ill but recuperating. As the nurse at Frey Martin had used up his supply of antibiotics, I treated her with tetracycline; also, I treated her mother, Rosa H., who had been sick for three days. We left Irazola at 7:00 A.M. on 14 June.

Arriving at Vencedor at 11:00 A.M., we confirmed reports received previously that the young former chief of the community, Antonio Lopez, age 35, had died on 29 May leaving a widow and several children. He became sick with diarrhea in the morning, went to work in his garden anyway, felt severe abdominal cramps at six in the evening, and died at 3:00 A.M. Lucía Limas Perez, a 21-year-old mother of three, died on June 7.

In Vencedor, I worked with Juan Manrique Alomías, chief of the community and previously health promoter, and César Rivas, current health promoter, to conduct health education and to find other cases as well as to do my research. One woman, Martha V., had become ill that morning, and I started her on antibiotic and rehydration treatment. She was better the next day. Carlos P. B., a boy of ten years, had become ill the day before and looked to me to be seriously dehydrated and somewhat listless even though he was alert and active. He was being cared for by his grandmother since his mother and father were in the camp downriver where we had found Alfonso. I began antibiotic and hydration treatment for Carlos, and he was better the next day.

We completed the work in Vencedor at 11:00 A.M. the next day, 15 June, and left for Tupac Amaru. We arrrived at Tupac at 1:30 P.M.

At Tupac Amaru we were received by one the health promoters, Julio Mera, with the sad news that my friend and senior health promoter, Elén Pérez, had died on 8 June, a few days after his wife, Rosa Lomas Flores. There had been various cases of cholera whom Julio had saved and who had been saved by the new Health Department *sanitario*[2] assigned to Charashmanan, Segundo Soria.

---

1 Health promoter" *(promotor de salud)*—lay health worker and community health officer

2 *Sanitario*—medical corpsman or practical nurse

These cases included Oscar L., sixty years of age, and his wife, Llaquelina C., and Roger V., twenty years of age.

At 3:00 P.M. the next day, 16 June, we left Tupac Amaru and arrived after a few minutes in Charashmanan, a community of approximately 350 people. Charashmanan has a health promoter, Ruperto Linares. The state sanitario for the special cholera program, Segundo Soria Bartra, arrived in Charashmanan on 9 June to fight the epidemic. Although there had been more than fifty cases of cholera in Charashmanan with seven deaths during the previous month, there were no deaths after the arrival of Sr. Soria. The dead include:

Jorge Lima Linares	22 years	d. 17 May 1991
Simeon Ruiz Odicio	50 years	d. 2 June 1991
Rafael Velasco Rios	38 years	d. 20 May 1991
Rosalía Perez Ruiz	36 years	d. 3 June 1991
Francisca Linares Gratelly	25 years	d. 3 June 1991
Roberta Saldaña Gomez	18 years	d. 23 May 1991
Geroncio Vega Acho	65 years	d. 1 June 1991

Rafael and Rosalía Perez were married and left two orphans. Roberta was the sister of Alfonso who died in the camp. All the young adults left surviving children.

Charashmanan was the most devastated, but the work of Srs. Linares and Soria saved many lives.

In Manco Capac, according to the information we had, there was one death due to cholera, the Doña D.A., but we could not confirm this directly. We do not have any information from the other communties on the Pisqui.

Since he had used up most of his materials for intravenous treatment and almost all his antibiotics, I gave some materials and the rest of my tetracycline to Sr. Soria. Also, I sent some intravenous materials and antibiotics of my own to the state sanitario in Nuevo Eden, Sr. Julio Linares, Lima. I also sent a bag of antibiotics from my own office and oral rehydration salts to Sr. Edwin Valera, health promoter in Manco Capac.

With this, we left Charashmanan on 17 June, stopping at all the communties to give small quantities of antibiotics and oral rehydration salts for the use of the health promoters until we got to the community of Ninth of October. We arrived at Paoyhän, some 50 kilometers up the river from the mouth of the Pisqui, at 10:30 P.M. that evening. On 19 June, we left Pao for Pucallpa at 8:00 A.M., camping on the beach downriver from San Pedro for the night and arriving at Yarinacocha at 11:30 A.M on 20 June.

Although we have no official information, we received a report from the Voz Nativa of Yarinacocha that 130 Shipibo had died in the Ucayali Basin, exclusive of those we had counted, for a minimum of 146.

Discussion

According to the information we had, there have been various instances of people traveling by "colectivo," or passenger boat, on the Ucalyai River who have died of cholera en route before arriving at their destinations. The excretions from these victims obviously enter the river. We do not know how many of the other passengers on these colectivos are exposed to cholera in these cases. But there are various means by which the distribution of cholera by the river could occur.

One instance of this that we know about is the death of Sr. Alberto Castro of Nuevo Saposoa, who became sick during his journey on the colectivo from Pucallpa to Nuevo Saposoa but died before arriving at his point of disembarkation, Tacshitea.

The hygienic conditions on many of the colectivos that use the Ucayali River are extremely poor and subhuman. Excrement from the toilets enters the river directly. The food preparation is usually contaminated. The colectivos and other craft are liberally floating epidemics.

Contamana, which reportedly has not itself had many cases of cholera, receives many cases from other communities at its hospital. Because of this, Contamana is a source of cholera for the Pisqui since many people from the Pisqui come there for their business or official activities.

On the upper Pisqui, there is a new community of religious cultists, the "Israelites," above the last native community of Nuevo Eden. These people come from Lima, the principal national source of the cholera epidemic.

The Shipibo have occupied the region of the Pisqui and lower Ucayali and have survived there well for a thousand years or more without boiling their water. Boiling it and observing strict hygiene for water and food is very difficult if not impossible in the conditions under which most of the Shipibo live—essentially camping. Unhappily, with new conditions of greatly increased human populations, some of the innocent customs may now be fatal. In addition, many of the Shipibo are severely compromised in their health by tuberculosis, intestinal parasites, and profound anemia due to both. They have little resistance to a virulent microbe such as cholera.

For my part, I appreciate the fact that the Ministry of Health and its professionals have worked hard against many difficulties to overcome this threat to the people of Perú.

INTERSECTION EMERGENCY

911 Operator:
Hello. What's your emergency?

Concerned citizen:
Well, it isn't one yet, but the traffic light at the intersection of Pine Street and Broadway is stuck. It doesn't change.

911 Operator:
Is it stuck on red or green?

Concerned citizen:
It depends on which way you're going.

BIOLOGICAL TYRANNY

T HE SITE THAT ELEANOR ROOSEVELT visited in West Virginia
during the Depression and described as the poorest place in America is still,
according to local inhabitants, as miserable as ever, if not worse. The mountains, long denuded of their finest timber, are heavily eroded and gouged by
strip mines. They look like partly plucked and badly butchered chickens. Their
topsoil is buried beneath the eviscerated hillsides or silted into black streams
choked with coal dust and sulfuric acid. An ugly industrial slum winds through
the valleys from Huntington to Charleston and is overlain with a yellowish-
grey pall which impartially dissolves lung tissue and automobile finish. The
rivers are a stinking cauldron of industrial poisons.

Into this mutilated landscape the newly born miner's child is thrust. The
mother, battered by repeated childbearing, struggles against sheer physical ex-
haustion. Years in the mines have left the father with a chronic cough, frequent
chest pain, shortness of breath, and other symptoms of severe lung disease and
early heart failure. If he is lucky enough to have a job at all in the mines, he
may earn as little as $2.75 per each car loaded with 1 to 1-$1/2$ tons of coal; and
he loads seven cars a day in a 12- to 14-hour day. The work is dangerous and
sporadic. In the smaller mines, he buys his own equipment. There are no fringe
benefits. The coal is sold for up to $12 a ton to others, or perhaps slightly less if
he buys it to heat his own tumbledown shack. The shack has no running water,
sanitation, or privacy. When it is available, electricity powers a few naked light
bulbs and, if work has been steady recently, perhaps a new refrigerator. Except
for a TV and a telephone that works only occasionally, the refrigerator is the
only appliance. For this the miner pays "so much a month"—perhaps up to
four times the real retail price.

To the south of West Virginia, the strip mines are invading the beautiful
Smoky Mountains of eastern Tennessee, and the inhabitants are becoming
impoverished in an environment unfit for humans.

On a crisp, sunny November morning, I stood in the littered front yard of
a Tennessee mountain family's household talking with Robert Brooks of Oak
Ridge. Brooks is a 45-year-old chemical plant worker who became so

enthusiastic about his wife's activities as an OEO family-planning outreach worker that he decided to help in his spare time. Brooks is a poor coal miner's son from one of the remote "hollers" of Tennessee.

We had come to visit one of the poorest families near the unemployment-stricken village of Fratersville, and we stood well out in the yard waiting to be invited in. We looked across the valley at the fading but still splendid autumn foliage and watched as a strip mining operation ripped a brown, ragged wound across the hillside. A few days before, water accumulating from heavy rains had broken through some of these abandoned shelves, unleashing a destructive flash flood on the hollow near Fratersville.

A woman finally asked us to come in. She invited us to sit on a tattered sofa in a room otherwise barren except for a potbelly iron stove and a broken wooden chair. She pulled the chair near the glowing stove and sat down. As we talked, she slumped forward and watched her children listlessly, her arms crossed. She spoke in a monotone. She was thirty-eight years old. She and her husband had nine living children. She was six months pregnant. "I tuck them pills for awhile, but my stumick got to botherin' me like it did afor I tuck 'em so I quit for three months. Couldn't afford 'em, no how." Brooks told her that she could get free medical exams and birth control help at the OEO clinic, and she said, "Well, I'll be down after the baby's got borned, but ain't there some way asides a pill?"

Similar requests from families with all the children they want are commonly heard by Brooks and his fellow OEO outreach workers in Tennessee. Mrs. Jeanette Smith, the nurse directing the OEO-funded Anderson County Family Planning Project through the local Planned Parenthood organization, estimates that her office receives four to five sterilization requests a week from poor families. A recent program-management survey of OEO family planning projects, which are currently serving more than 300,000 patients, indicates that this is far from unusual. Eighty percent of the projects reported that they wanted to provide sterilization as part of their regular services, which already include pelvic exams, cancer detection, VD screening, counseling, and education, as well as contraceptives and referral for other medical problems. Project directors such as Mrs. Smith, however, feel that many of the patients want sterilization and that a complete program should include this service. Perhaps the most surprising aspect of this experience in Tennessee is the frequency of requests by men for vasectomy, the male sterilizing operation. In his contacts with the mountain men of Tennessee, Robert Brooks makes no secret of the fact that he had a vasectomy done after he and his wife had their child fifteen years ago. Since vasectomy cannot now be offered by OEO programs, he does not bring up the subject deliberately.

One man, a seasonally employed garage mechanic, wanted a vasectomy done on himself as soon as it could be arranged. He and his 26-year-old wife have three children. She has also had two miscarriages. She cannot take birth control pills because of chronic kidney disease, high blood pressure, chronic urinary tract infections, and rheumatic heart disease. Other forms of contraception have been ineffective or unsuitable for her. Yet she will be risking pregnancy for the next twenty years. Her last unplanned child was delivered by Caesarean section. Any future pregnancy would probably require a similar operation. Some of their medical bills are paid by public sources, but one more child would plunge them even deeper into debt.

Another woman in her early twenties, an outreach worker for one of the Tennessee family planning projects, is plagued by extreme obesity, made worse with each pregnancy. She weighs close to 300 pounds. The obesity is also aggravated by taking birth control pills, but she is so fearful of pregnancy she doesn't want to stop taking them. Her anxiety about pregnancy causes her to eat more and the problem gets worse. She and her husband have three children "... all we can handle. We don't want any more children." Her last pregnancy was unwanted. All three children have been ill and have had recent hospital stays. Her husband was seriously injured nearly a year ago and is unable to work. They want sterilization for either one but can't afford it.

As an outreach worker, she has found that many women are in situations similar to hers. She herself was unaware of the possibilities of help before she was contacted by an OEO outreach worker. "I knew that there was a pill, but I didn't know if I could get it until one of the volunteers came and told me about it."

A young woman in her late twenties told me that neither she nor her middle-aged unemployed husband, who has had two heart attacks, wants any more children. None of her three children was intended. Her first child was born out of wedlock; the others have been born since she married in 1968. She was using foam and the rhythm method, respectively, when she became pregnant with the last two. They came thirteen months apart. Her first thought, she says, when she discovered her last pregnancy, was "... how can I get rid of it?" They live in a cramped trailer house, and she says, "Each one makes it harder on the ones we already got. We couldn't really afford them, but here they are so what can you do?" She wants to be sterilized and "... would go this afternoon if I thought I could get it done," but they don't have the money to pay. Her youngest child is six months old.

A dejected, tobacco-chewing young man shifted nervously in front of a squat iron stove which provided the only heat for his one-room tarpaper shelter. He looked past his 31-year-old wife at one of their seven children, who was screaming and pummeling a younger brother, and said, "I git another I reckon I'll shoot myself." Their house burned down two years ago Christmas, and he has been unemployed "for a long time." He takes odd jobs and they get food surplus, but there seems to be no way to get ahead. Their "house" has no running water, toilet, or adequate cooking facilities; they have no refrigerator. His wife looks nearly twenty years older than her age. The youngest child is three months old. All the children are anemic and dirty. Two appear to be mentally retarded. The others go to school only when the weather is warm. They have no shoes or warm clothes. The man wants his hernia fixed and a vasectomy done at the same time. "We got all we kin handle." His wife became pregnant with their youngest child when she ran out of birth control pills and couldn't afford to buy more at the time. She was recently contacted by the local OEO family-planning outreach worker and has begun attending the clinic, but both she and her husband feel that temporary measures such as the "pill" are not enough to suit their need. However, they cannot afford an operation, which would cost around $100 for the man's vasectomy or as much as $400 for the woman.

Families like these need jobs, decent housing, a healthy environment, adequate food, clean water, sanitation, and education. OEO health programs, including the 450 projects primarily concerned with family planning, provide a network of services that are meeting some of these individual needs. But one of the most important needs is freedom from the tyranny of their own biology.

MISTER BROOKS

If they want to get down and pray,
I get down and pray with 'em.

If they want to sip whisky,
I sip whisky.

Sometimes

      we jis whittle.

EXAMINING THE SST PROJECT

TRANSPORTATION SECRETARY JOHN VOLPE's mindless eulogy of the Boeing SST project on June 5 reveals both his incompetence as a public official and the frightful momentum of stupid policies. Even more appalling than this was the recent approval by the House of Representatives of renewed funds for the SST.

It is inconceivable that the votes thereby gained for the Nixon administration and for the SST's congressional supporters can possibly outweigh the economic and ecological damage that would result from this absurd enterprise.

As a physician and as an epidemiologist, I am quite certain that the noise pollution effects in the path of the SST will have serious adverse effects on all living creatures with intact nervous systems. The meteorological and ecological effects that are predicted from currently available evidence spell disaster on a much broader scale.

As a non-represented resident of Washington, D.C., I resent being heavily taxed to finance a private business venture of less than doubtful merit to build an environment-destroying machine that will not only not be used in the U.S. (hopefully) but will, in any case, be beyond the benefit or use of the average citizen. This is even more tragic for our fellow citizens with low or marginal incomes, whose taxes also go for nothing.

The President and Mr. Volpe have given us the vague and specious excuse of national prestige as the reason for building the SST. This is a lot of hot air, to put it politely, even if what prestige we had were not being destroyed by our insane adventures in Southeast Asia.

No one stands to profit from this ghastly project but Boeing Aircraft, the petroleum industry, and somebody's political campaign treasury.

Even though I am not an economist, it is also easy to see that vast expenditures for non-investment toys like the SST are grave errors in the face of inflation, rising unemployment, and unchecked population growth. What we need, instead, are wise capital investments and careful mangement of our resources to provide for the increasingly desperate social, health, and educational needs of our people.

Secretary Volpe needs only to walk around the poorer districts of Washington to see the human needs with which those SST funds are competing. He needs only to spend several hours being asphyxiated in a traffic jam to understand that it is getting less and less possible to move in and out of our cities or even from one side of town to another.

In view of these many problems, there is not much to be said for getting to London or Paris two hours faster, assuming you can afford to go there. In any case, the traffic jams on both ends of the trip will cancel out the two hours "saved."

—Warren M. Hern, M.D.
  Washington

HAVE SOME MEDIOCRE BEER

ONE BEAUTIFUL SPRING AFTERNOON following a seminar at the University of Colorado, a colleague of mine and I decided to go downtown to have lunch at a popular Mexican restaurant with an outdoor patio. The waiter came to take our orders, and after we had chosen the dishes we wanted, he asked us if we wanted anything to drink.

"Do you have any dark beer?" I asked.

"No, but we have some mediocre beer," he replied.

"Why would I want mediocre beer?" I asked.

" Well, we don't have any dark beer, and the only other kind we have is light beer and something in between."

"What do you think *mediocre* means?" I asked the waiter.

"It means 'in the middle,'" he replied.

"Where did you go to school?" I asked.

"At _____ _____ (a school of higher education on the East Coast)," he replied.

"Young man, you have a *mediocre* education, and you have a *mediocre* command of the English language," I said.

"What do you mean?" he asked.

"Because *mediocre* doesn't mean in the middle; it means lousy, not very good, inferior," I said.

"It does not. Not in my dictionary. In my dictionary, it means *in the middle*, like, *in between* dark beer and light beer."

"In that case," I said, "you have a *mediocre* dictionary, and you ought to think about getting a new one."

He brought me a Dos Equis beer with my enchiladas, and we had a nice lunch. I even gave him a good tip so he could make a down payment on a better dictionary.

HAPPY 90TH BIRTHDAY, EDNA

E DNA HERN, my mother, was born on April 4, 1917 in Salina, Kansas. When she was born, World War I was being fought, the Russian Revolution was beginning, and Woodrow Wilson was President. She cast her first vote ever for Franklin Roosevelt in 1940. Roosevelt's fireside chats and leadership in the Great Depression gave hope to her and to my father, John. They cried on the day Roosevelt died. I remember it.

When my mother was one year old, her mother, a very beautiful young woman, died in the influenza epidemic of 1918, leaving my mother, her older sister Audrey, and her brother Eustace, in the care of her father, Wiley. My grandfather Wiley had left the family homestead in the remote hills of North Carolina to seek his fortune out West. After working for a time as a shopkeeper, sheepherder, and postmaster of Rock Springs, Wyoming, at around the turn of the century, he went to Salina to court and marry my grandmother. He had met her on the train while going home to visit his family in North Carolina. Wiley worked twelve hours a day in the Salina flour mill lifting 160-pound sacks of flour. He didn't make much money. The kids, especially after my grandmother's death, had to be pretty self-reliant. Wiley made oatmeal for the kids at 5:00 A.M. and arranged for their care before going to the mill, but after that, they had to learn how to do a lot of things themselves. My mom carried a lot of water (and ice, in the hot Kansas summers).

When my mother was 14, she walked out of a Baptist Sunday school class because she didn't believe what the preacher was saying about dancing and playing cards being sinful. She liked music and dancing and enjoyed playing cards with her friends and family, so she decided to get up and leave. In Salina, Kansas in 1931, this was a singular act of intellectual and personal independence. She didn't go to college, but at Salina High School she studied Latin, French, music, and literature.

My mother met my father, who was from Abilene, at a dance. They got married in 1935. It was the height (or depth) of the Depression. It was hard to make a living, but they were both resourceful and hard workers. Two months after Pearl Harbor they got on the train with me and moved to Colorado to find work and have a better future for their kids. They had $3.50 when they arrived at Union Station in Denver.

During the war, when my father was building piers and military installations in Alaska, my mother made sandwiches for United Airlines' Sky Chef Service while my Grandpa Hern stood on ladders and pumped gas into DC-3's at Stapleton Airport. We had a Victory Garden, and we saved scrap metal for the war effort. She got me through rheumatic fever when I was six (no antibiotics yet) and, several years later, an enormous, dangerous, and very uncomfortable boil on my ass from a chigger bite (still no antibiotics) that I got while visiting my cousin on the farm in Kansas. She cured it with hot flax-seed poultices several times a day. She understood a basic principle of surgery.

Since those days, my mother has seen World War II, ended finally by the atomic bomb; the introduction of sulfa and penicillin; the breakup of European empires; the establishment of the United Nations, the eradication of smallpox and polio; the Berlin Airlift; the Marshall Plan; the beginning of television broadcasts, jet airplanes, turn signals, automatic transmissions, transistor chips, computers, and the Internet; the Korean War; the Cold War; McCarthyism; the Cuban Missile Crisis; the civil rights movement; Vietnam; the women's liberation movement; the fall of the Berlin Wall, the collapse of the Soviet Union; the Gulf War; and now, the Iraq War. Presidents Harding, Coolidge, Hoover, Roosevelt, Truman, Eisenhower, Kennedy, Johnson, Nixon, Ford, Carter, Reagan, Bush 41, and Clinton have come and gone. She thinks George W. Bush is the worst, stupidest, most ignorant, most dangerous, and most destructive of them all. She has a definite opinion about this. She's a nice, quiet, 90-year-old grandmother who will offer you incredibly delicious, addictive hot banana bread and cinnamon rolls, but she will tell you her opinion about political matters if you ask and really want to know.

Before I was a year old, my mother began reading me poetry and nursery rhymes. She and my dad bought me an encyclopedia—*The Book of Knowledge*—and my mother read to me from it for hours, so I learned to read before I started school. My mother never heard the phrase "quality time," but my sisters and I got it in large quantities.

My mother raised three kids on a carpenter's income, but since there were very few things that she or my father couldn't make or fix or grow, we never felt poor. My sisters and I never felt deprived, and we did a lot of things together as a family. We went sledding and ice-skating in the winter, we had picnics by the mountain streams in the summer, and we would walk from Englewood to Cheesman Park in Denver for concerts. My mom took me on the streetcar down to the Denver Auditorium to see the original stage production of *Porgy and Bess* when I was five. I remember it vividly. They bought me books and a piano for $25 on that carpenter's pay in 1944, and they paid for piano lessons with Miss Owens. They suffered through hours and days and years of practice and came to all my recitals. My mother was a Cub Scout Den Mother for me

and my friends. Both my mother and father were active in the Methodist Church. When the daughter of friends got married, my dad gave all the seats and fixtures in the church sanctuary a new paint job for the wedding.

When I was about 12, I captured a large toad out in the field behind the back yard and decided to see how long it would live under water. After the toad was certifiably dead, I cut it open to see what its organs were like. Then I decided to stuff the toad with rags, and I sewed it up with string and a large needle borrowed from my mother. Then I was inspired to place the toad, looking nearly alive, in a crouching position at eye level on top of a stack of cement sacks my dad had placed just inside the garage door. When my mother opened the door and walked inside the dark garage the next morning, she came face-to-face with the stuffed toad. It was a bad moment in Edna's life.

In 1952, my mother took me to Stapleton Airport to see Dwight Eisenhower as he was campaigning for President. She encouraged me to go to the Photography Club in junior high school. My dad built me a darkroom in the basement utility room. In 1956, my photograph of a high jumper from our school won second prize in the Kodak National High School Snapshot Contest. In 1987, my photograph of a South American jaguar was on the cover of the *Sierra Club Wildlife Calendar*. My mother helped make that happen.

Early in high school my mother knew I was interested in being a doctor, and that I admired Albert Schweitzer, so she took me to an Open House at the CU Medical School. It was unforgettable. Going into the microbiology lab was almost a religious experience for me. I had read about Hippocrates, Lister,

Pasteur, Vesalius, Galen, Harvey, Hunter, Edward Jenner, and all the great doctors of history. It is a great tradition. My mother encouraged me to follow it. She and my dad were there when I graduated from medical school in 1965, and they were also at the graduation ceremony in North Carolina when I received my Ph.D. in epidemiology in 1988.

In the fall of 1960, my mother and I went to the Greek Theatre in the Denver Civic Center to see John F. Kennedy give a speech as he ran for President. It was an electric, inspiring, unforgettable experience.

In 1967, I brought my mother and father and two sisters to Brazil where I was working as a Peace Corps physician. I met them in Manaus on the Amazon, and from there we traveled to Belem, Fortaleza, Recife, and Salvador, where I was on duty. We went to Rio and saw Corcovado, Pão de Açucar, Ipanema, and Copacabana, then on to São Paulo, to the Falls of Iguaçu, to Lima, Peru, to Machu Picchu, Ollantaytambo, Pisac, and back to Lima before they went home. My parents had never been out of the United States. For my mother and father, it was the trip of a lifetime.

My father, her partner for 54 years, died in 1990. It was very hard for her. Later, she met Wayne, who was uncannily like my father—a vigorous, independent tradesman, outdoorsman, and craftsman—but with all of my father's virtues and few of his defects. They were sweethearts, giggling and holding hands. Wayne was devoted to my mother and she to him. They enjoyed their life together. They traveled, played cribbage, entertained friends and family, and told each other stories. Some of my mother's old friends were scandalized that she and Wayne weren't married. "Now, slow down, sweetie," he would say from his observation post in the front passenger seat, as my mother lead-footed it through western Kansas, chickens and farmers fleeing for safety. Wayne was nicer than the State Patrol.

Wayne died a few years ago, and it was a terrible loss for my mother. Now she spends a lot of time with her lady friends playing cards, sewing, and talking politics. This is a radical bunch. Bill Clinton is hot. How could somebody as dumb as George Bush get to be President? Isn't Nancy great?

On Sunday mornings my mother will call me up and say, "Did you hear what Dick Cheney [or whoever else is on] just said to Tim Russert?" "Yes, Mother." "That guy is so full of it!" (That's a gentle translation for readers of a family newspaper.)

Mother is worried about global warming, the war in Iraq, democracy and civil liberties in our country, the increasing coarseness and decline in civility and integrity in American society, the national debt, the economy, standards of education for children, and women's rights. The human population has quadrupled in her lifetime. She is one of the few persons in three million years of human evolution and history to be witness to such a cataclysmic change in human experience. "How are all those people going to get by?" she asks.

About a month ago, my mother met Nancy Pelosi, the first woman Speaker of the United States House of Representatives. I introduced my mother to Nancy as a 90-year-old Franklin Roosevelt New Deal Great Depression Democrat. It was a great moment for both women.

Women couldn't vote when my mother was born. Things have changed in ninety years.

SOUTH AMERICAN JAGUAR (PANTHERA ONÇA), MANU NATIONAL PARK

Having visited Manu in 1984, I returned for an extended photographic expedition in 1985. After having camped out and gone to a blind to take photographs of macaws earlier in the day, we were returning to the main camp downstream when I saw this jaguar lying on a tree that had fallen across a small stream flowing from the riverbank across from us. I had the Machiguenga boatmen turn the canoe around and come to rest on a small sandbar delta of the stream. We were about 15 meters from the jaguar. He (she?—I didn't do an inspection) watched me carefully as I climbed out of the canoe onto the sandbar and set up my camera on a tripod while hoping that a) the jaguar would not come after me, b) would not run away, c) I would not sink into quicksand.

This was one of the first two or three pictures I took. The jaguar was still there watching me, three rolls of film later, when we decided to leave because it was getting dark. It was starting to rain, the mosquitoes were horrible, and we had to get back to camp.

When we got home a month later, I called the *Sierra Club Calendar* editors, who were holding several other of my previously submitted photographs, and told them that I had a superb picture of a South American jaguar in the wild. I told them that I would hold it for next year's submission. "Where's the picture," the editor asked. "Right here," I replied. "How soon can you send it to me?" she asked. "Tomorrow," I replied. I had a copy made the next day and sent the original by FedEx. A week later, the editor called me to tell me that they were going to put it on the cover of the 1987 *Sierra Club Wildlife Calendar*. At the request of Charlie Munn, the Princeton ornithologist who helped arrange for my stay in Manu National Park, I made a large poster of the photograph. The poster was used to raise money for Wildlife Conservation International. It later appeared on the cover of the dust jacket of a book, *Celebration of Life*, published in Mexico, which was a collection of the best wildlife photographs available at the time. It is certainly the best and most memorable wildlife photograph I have taken.

155

THE BIRDS OF LOUISIANA

Sᴡᴇᴇᴛ ᴀʀᴇ ᴛʜᴇ ᴜsᴇs ᴏғ ᴀᴅᴠᴇʀsɪᴛʏ. One day in 1978, while waiting to see a neurosurgeon for a neck injury, I spotted an *Audubon* magazine anniversary issue with a spectacularly beautiful bird photograph on the cover. As I reviewed the issue, I found photographs by Philip Kahl, a zoologist and accomplished photographer, that took my breath away. The most striking pictures were of roseate spoonbills in the swamps of Louisiana. There was also a picture of the photographer standing by some of his subjects.

As I knew I was going to Louisiana soon to take board exams in preventive medicine, I decided to get a telephoto lens or two that I needed and try to photograph these birds. I managed to get a 400mm telephoto lens at a highly discounted price from a friend in Panama who had one of the best camera shops anywhere. I found Dr. Kahl, got some advice from him, and then called John O'Neill, an ornithologist at the LSU museum in Baton Rouge. John advised me to go to Avery Island, which turns out to be a bird sanctuary built by the patriarchs of the McIlhenny family, producers of Tabasco Sauce. This family had owned a series of islands on the Louisiana delta since before the Civil War and had made its fortune, first, with hot sauce made from peppers imported from Mexico, then salt, which was found in underground domes under the islands, then oil. One of the family seniors, alarmed at around the end of the nineteenth century with the rapid disappearance of the beautiful wading birds in the area, decided to build a bird sanctuary. He went to India to consult an Indian maharaja who had done this, then came back and created a sanctuary at Avery Island. It is also a garden museum of plants from all over the world.

So I went to Avery Island for a few days and started photographing. Then I went back another time, this time renting a little car and driving down to the coast and inner bayous. At one point I found myself by the Rockefeller Wildlife Refuge. No one was in the office except the janitor, who told me to call back the following week. I did, and the biologist with whom I spoke told me that I could find out where to take pictures of roseate spoonbills from a man named John Richard, a Cajun saloonkeeper in Grand Chenier, in Cameron Parish. So, I found the telephone number for John's Bar and Grill in Grand Chenier.

"John's Bar and Grill," in a deeply Southern accent; voices, clinking glasses, the sound of billiards clicking in the background, male voices nearby.

Using the Cajun pronunciation of his last name, I said, "May I speak to John Richard, please?"

"Who're you?"

"I'm Dr. Warren Hern. I'm calling from Colorado."

"Where?"

"Colorado."

Pause.

"What's yer bidness?"

"I want to take pictures of some birds, and people down the road at the wildlife refuge told me that John could tell me where to find them."

"What? Birds?"

"Yeah, roseate spoonbills."

Glasses clinking, billiard shots breaking in the background. Pause.

"You wanna talk to John about rosy egrets?"

"Yeah, that's all I want."

Long pause. Billiard shots in the background.

(new voice) "Hello."

"Is this John Richard?"

"Yeah. Who're you?"

"I'm Dr. Warren Hern. I'm in Colorado, but I want to come take pictures of roseate spoonbills, and the people at the wildlife refuge told me you could help me find 'em."

"Yeah, well, you need to talk to my son, Armand. He lives out there by the river. He knows where they are."

Soon after, I spoke to Armand, an oil-rig roughneck living on the edge of the bayou. Armand was very friendly, and when I told him what I wanted he said he would help me. I said I would fly into Lake Charles, get a car, and drive to his house. He insisted on coming to Lake Charles to get me, which he did. He met me at the airport, introduced me to his family in the car, bought two six-packs of beer, and started out for his house. Armand and his family lived in a little house right on the riverbank. For the occasion, he invited his parents and his friend Glen over, and they put on a fish fry for me. Armand gave me a place to sleep in a trailer near the house. He carefully lit mosquito-coils before leaving me to sleep. We got up before dawn the next day and loaded my stuff in a boat with an outboard motor. With Glen, we set out on the Mermentau River.

As dawn broke, we approached a small island that was teeming with thousands of birds. They were silhouetted against the dawn sky and rising sun as we landed. After unloading my gear, Armand and Glen got ready to go. "We'll come back to pick you up this afternoon." "No, if you don't mind, I'd like for you to pick me up tomorrow morning." They could not believe that I planned to camp on this birdshit-covered island that was about a fourth the size of a football field. "I'll be fine, and I can take pictures from my tent in the morning," I reassured them.

The island, which was a shell midden left by native Americans, was covered by low brush including mangrove bushes, and there must have been twenty or thirty thousand birds on it. There were great egrets, snowy egrets, cattle egrets, herons, roseate spoonbills, cormorants, and anhingas. There may have been other species that I did not see. There were nests everywhere. I set up my tent and put my view camera in it, then set up my 35mm camera with various telephoto lenses. The birds were so close that I didn't need a telephoto lens with many pictures. I moved slowly and carefully, and the birds didn't seem to be disturbed.

As dawn broke the next day, I poked my camera lens out the opening and took pictures of anything I could see. After awhile, I ran out of film for my 35mm camera and set up my view camera. I don't know how many people have taken 4 x 5 view camera pictures of roseate spoonbill chicks in the nest, but it was the last picture I took on the island with the last piece of film. Then I waited for Armand and Glen to come get me, which they did about noon.

I sent the family a copy of my best spoonbill picture, which was published in the *Sierra Club Engagement Calendar* in 1989.

The town of Grand Chenier was wiped out by Hurricane Rita on September 24, 2005. The storm surge that swept over the town was fifteen feet deep.

THE DEATH MARCH
IN GLACIER NATIONAL PARK

FROM THE TIME WE FIRST MET at a medical conference in Denver in 1972, Jim Armstrong and I were friends. Jim is a soft-spoken, deliberate, conscientious person practicing medicine in Kalispell, Montana. He is a family doctor, one of the best, and the kind of person who holds communities together. He was a Boy Scout leader, a member of the school board, a leader in his church, and a courageous defender of women's rights in a conservative, rural area.

When I visited him in Kalispell on a tour of family planning clinics in the Rocky Mountain states as a consultant for a federal program, we hit it off and discovered that we both loved the outdoors and backpacking in wilderness areas. I missed a couple of chances to go in the back country with him and his friends, but we finally agreed to do a long trip in Glacier National Park. During various phone conversations, we agreed on who would carry the food, the tent, the stove, utensils, and other survival gear. We would start at Lower Kintla Lake and come out at the bottom of Bowman Lake. Just before I was to leave for Montana, I asked him how far our "loop" would be through Hole-in-the-Wall Basin. "About forty miles," Jim said. "But Jim, we only have four days. That's ten miles a day, and I will be carrying a heavy pack with a lot of camera gear. We are going over two passes. I think we ought to find a way to cut that distance in half." "Okay," he said. He called back and said he had figured out a route for twenty miles. "That's more like it," I said. "I love to do this, but I'm not a masochist."

Jim's kids drove us to the trailhead at the outlet of Lower Kintla Lake. Eleven miles later, we reached the campground at the upper end of Upper Kintla Lake just as it was getting dark. I was carrying a pack of about eighty pounds, at least forty-five pounds of which was camera gear. I had a 4 x 5 view camera, several lenses for it, six 4 x 5 film holders, a drape cloth for viewing, a film changing bag, a heavy tripod, filters, and other paraphernalia needed for this setup. I also had two heavy Canon F-1 35mm camera bodies, five lenses (including a 400mm telephoto) for these cameras, and twenty rolls of 35mm film. It was all I could do to add a sleeping bag, sleeping pad, my part of the survival gear, and clothes. When we crossed a stretch of stone by Lower Kintla Lake, the depressions in the rock made by my footsteps were visible behind me. I was exhausted when we made our first camp.

As we hiked the next day our way up over a thousand feet of elevation to Boulder Pass, which we were to cross during the day before dropping down to

camp in Hole-in-the-Wall Basin, it was apparent that Jim and I had very different ways of approaching the trip. I wanted to take a picture of every rock, flower, bug, animal, and view; Jim wanted to run through the forest with a thirty-pound pack, scaring all the animals out of the way so we could get through quickly.

By the time we got to Boulder Pass, however, Jim was the one who gave out. He couldn't go any further. So we camped illegally on Boulder Pass, which turned out in the morning to be one of the most beautifully spectacular places on the planet. Jim slept with his .357 Magnum "bear repellant" under his pillow since we were off the trail and in grizzly country. I got up at dawn, set up my view camera, and got a "lifer"—one the best pictures in my life as a photographer—a view of a small tarn on the pass looking down the valley far below into Brown's Pass.

On the third day (now clearly beyond the promised twenty miles), we hiked down into Hole-in-the-Wall Basin, where we were to have legally camped the night before. We pushed on around the narrow trail carved into a 2,000-foot cliff and down to the Brown's Pass campground, where we had a permit to camp on the third night. But the Brown's Pass campground was clearly set up for Backpackers Who Had Sinned on the Trail. The mosquitoes were so horrible it was hard to breath. So we kept talking down into the valley above Bowman Lake. We nervously pitched our tents on a gravel bar in the middle of the river and hoped it wouldn't rain and that we wouldn't be found by the grizzly bears.

The next morning we hiked several miles on down to Bowman Lake, where we made breakfast on a brilliant sunny day. I could barely walk, and we had another eight miles to go. My feet were covered with blisters. At the end, we had covered about forty miles.

When I got to my office in Colorado the next day, my staff told me that Jim had called them to say they should meet me at the airport with crutches and a wheelchair. He thought he was being funny. In Montana, you get your entertainment from tormenting tenderfoot backpackers.

Jim's original print of my best picture from that trip hung in the waiting room of his medical practice until his office was fire-bombed and destroyed about fifteen years later by anti-abortion fanatics. I made a new copy of the picture for him for his birthday.

ENCOUNTERS WITH ELIOT PORTER

In 1978, when I realized that I really had to do something about my renewed passion for photography, I found out about a photo workshop in New Mexico with several leading natural history photographers, especially Jim Bones. Jim had been Eliot Porter's principal assistant for several years, and I admired his work.

The workshop, in a remote private ranch called Vermejo Park west of Raton Pass, lasted for about five days. Jim and I became great friends, I learned a lot, and I got some good pictures. I especially worked on my 4 x 5 view camera landscape technique.

In the process, Jim told me a lot about Eliot Porter, one of my heroes in photography and the great master of color photography. Eliot's 1962 master-piece, *In Wildness is the Preservation of the World*, was the Sierra Club's first large format publication of great wilderness and natural history photographs. Eliot chose a collection of writings by Henry David Thoreau (from which the title is taken) to accompany his photographs after David Brower, the first Executive Director of the Sierra Club, saw an exhibition of Porter's work at the Smithsonian Institution. The American tradition of natural history landscape color photography flows from Eliot's inspired work and vision.

I was intrigued by Jim's stories of working for Eliot. It involved working in Eliot's lab from dawn until dusk for months at a time making dye transfer color prints. This is a complicated process that involves making three black-and-white negatives from the original color transparency. Each negative contains information from one part of the color spectrum. These negatives are then used to make mats that hold the opposite color after being dipped in that dye. The mats are laid down, one after another, so that the colors combine and make the color print. It was the state of the art of color printing at the time. Eliot had helped Eastman Kodak develop the process in the early 1940s. Before going to medical school, Eliot had graduated from Harvard and Oxford in chemical engineering. He combined his scientific training with artistic genius to produce the finest photographic color prints of birds and landscape scenes in the world.

One day after returning from the workshop, I decided to call Eliot to see if I could speak with him. He answered the phone, and I told him that he had in-spired my efforts to capture the beauty of the Colorado wilderness with my view camera. I knew he was a physician, and I told him of my medical work and my research in the Amazon. He was very interested in both. We talked for an

hour. I couldn't believe it. Then we corresponded. I went to his home in Tesuque, New Mexico to visit him and get acquainted. I took some of my best wildlife and landscape photographs.

Eliot looked at my portfolio carefully, and said, "Hmmm," in the careful, studied manner of a psychiatrist who has just been told by his patient that the patient had committed an ax murder. It was the reaction of someone who has been professionally trained not to react too much to appalling information. I think Eliot did not want to discourage me. He showed me his studio, gave me an original print of one of the photographs in *In Wildness*, and signed my copy of his book. I left with my treasure and renewed inspiration, and we kept in touch.

Tesuque, New Mexico, is a long way in physical and cultural distance from Eliot's early Illinois and New England life experience. His father was a famous architect, and the family owned an island off the coast of Maine. Eliot's first book, *Penobscot Island*, captured some of the charm and history of that place. Even though educated as a chemist and physician, Eliot's first love was photography. He left a promising career in the Harvard laboratory of the great microbiologist, Hans Zinnser, to follow that passion. After recognition by a master photographer Alfred Stieglitz, and a Guggenheim fellowship, Eliot took his family from the secure, aristocratic environment that he knew and moved to the Native American milieu of northern New Mexico. "I didn't think I could accomplish anything with my life as a doctor or medical scientist," he said.

On May 19, 1980, the day that Mt. Saint Helens erupted, I happened to be visiting Eliot. We had spent the morning looking through some of his portfolios and discussing his philosophy of photographing the natural world. This he would call an "intimate landscape," in which he attempted to capture the beauty and wonder of the place in a portrait of a small portion of it. An exhibit of Eliot's work at the Metropolitan Museum of Art, "The Intimate Landscape," reflected this idea.

Over lunch, we watched the unfolding spectacle of Mt. Saint Helens and reflected on the forces of nature vs. the forces of the human species. We both deplored what humans are doing to destroy the natural world. I explained to him my idea that the human species has all the major characteristics of a malignant process. "It's too simple," he said. "It can't be that simple." But we agreed that humanity is on a frighteningly destructive path. "Man is an apparition," Eliot said. "We won't last. We appeared suddenly, and we will disappear." This brought reflections on war and its destructiveness. Eliot had seen World War I, World War II, the Korean War, and Vietnam in his lifetime. He became angry thinking about them, especially the first and the last. "What good is a tank?" he asked. "It's only good for killing people."

I took Eliot and his wife out to dinner in Santa Fe, and he regaled me with stories about his trips across North America as a medical student and his photographic expedition into Glen Canyon with David Brower before the Glen Canyon Dam was constructed. One of his best and favorite photographs was made after he swam up a small inlet into the canyon pushing his camera equipment on a float bag just ahead of him. We swapped wilderness stories for a long time. We talked until his wife Alene started to fall asleep.

Earlier in the day, Eliot took me into his studio and lab. We talked about his philosophy of photography and the discipline he applied to his work. We also talked about the dye transfer process and how he made the color separation negatives. Jim had argued with him about developing each negative by itself to get the best result or, as Eliot insisted on doing it, in batches. I had the temerity to ask Eliot about this technical point. He turned to me and crisply asked, with a little smile on his face, "How long do you have to live?"

The last time I saw Eliot was on April 5, 1989. He was very ill and could barely move, but he was working on five new books. I gave him a gentle hug, kissed him on the forehead, and told him that I loved him. Eliot was very reserved and didn't seem to be a demonstrative person, but I wanted him to know that. I didn't think he would mind. "Thank you," he said weakly. He died the next year.

EULOGY FOR FRED PRAEGER AT HIS MEMORIAL SERVICE

A GREAT SPIRIT HAS PASSED FROM OUR MIDST, one perhaps unknown to many in Boulder, but he has helped shape our world. The great privilege, however, was to know him in person—to know his warmth, blunt charm, acerbic wit, and stubborn irascibility. Fred Praeger was my friend, and knowing him was a singular honor in my life. I cherish the long conversations I had with him and Kellie at their kitchen table and at dinner and the candid, funny, and sometimes wise advice that Fred gave me. His advice was variously about physical fitness, politics, writing, publishing, and about my love life, in which he took a keen and concerned interest. Fred gave me, shall we say, his unvarnished opinions. We had no boring conversations.

Going to see *Schindler's List* with Fred and talking with him afterward about his family was one of the profoundly moving and unforgettable experiences of my life.

Fred was a champion athlete, a World War II freedom fighter who lost his parents to the Nazi ovens, a daring and innovative publisher, and an independent spirit who refused to let advancing age and illness keep him from enjoying his life. In the end, he stubbornly refused to accept an imposed twilight existence. To those of us who loved him, he remained a compelling and intriguing person who alternately drove us from fury to devotion and back to pure admiration.

For most, including those who will never be aware, the effects of Fred's life will be in how he shaped the history of our century. If you have noticed what has happened to Eastern Europe and the Soviet Union during the past thirty years, you should know that Fred played an immense and probably incalculable role in making that happen. Fred brought forth the ideas that changed that part of the world and with it, all of history.

The first serious book that I bought as a college student at the University of Colorado in 1950s was *The New Class*, Milovan Djilas's historic critique of the communist system that he had helped install in Yugoslavia. It was one of the first real cracks in the Iron Curtain, and it was followed by other books by Djilas (*Anatomy of a Moral, Conversations with Stalin*, etc.). Fred Praeger, working with borrowed money, founded Praeger Publishing Company in 1950. In a brilliant stroke of planning and intrigue, he worked with Djilas to obtain the *New Class* manuscript and publish it in the free air of the West.

The New Class was just the beginning. Fred went on to become a major publisher, not just through his original company and his Boulder creation, Westview Press, and not just by bringing forth an occasional brilliant work like those of Djilas and the historic *One Day in the Life of Ivan Denisovitch*, but by encouraging and publishing the works of a large group of brilliant authors who sought to express a vital set of ideas. Fred had a vision, and the most important part of that vision was freedom. Fred knew that facts are fatal to tyranny, and he knew that totalitarianism cannot withstand free thought. Fred was a midwife of not just one author or one important book but to the expression of freedom in his lifetime. The result is that our world has more freedom, justice, and liberty for more people than it had when he found it and as he knew it. That is his legacy to us.

Fred also published the works of major artists and brought them to public attention more than would have been possible if their creations were visible only in museums and galleries.

For those of us who love freedom, who think ideas are important, and who believe that published words may be the only permanent thing in the universe, Fred's passing gives us not merely personal grief but cause for serious reflection. It is not so clear that the economics and competitiveness of contemporary publishing will continue to permit the kind of success and intellectual freedom brought to us by this cantankerous and single-minded maverick.

What Fred achieved in his life, the publication of thousands of vital books that changed history, also makes us reflect on the power of ideas, and in particular, the power of the idea of freedom. Fred himself was, in his personal as well as professional life, one of the purest expressions of that idea. I miss him.

FLING'S FLUNG

I feel like a summer fling

Who has been flung.

GETTING ROLFED
IN WASHINGTON

ONE OF THE THINGS THAT I ENJOY most about practicing medicine is getting to know my patients. I chat with them and find out about their lives. It helps me establish a relationship of trust; it helps me find out important things about their lives that might affect their health issues; it's sometimes very interesting, and it's often fun. But sometimes my sense of curiosity and openness to new ideas gets me in trouble.

Not long after I started practicing medicine in Boulder, I saw a woman who told me in the course of our conversation while I was treating her that she and her husband had a "rolfing" business. I was new to Boulder, and, in fact, I had only returned recently from a long absence from the United States, so I had never heard of "rolfing." So I asked her what this was.

The patient very cheerfully told me that "rolfing" was a new kind of very intensive massage therapy that involved, apparently, a lot of force and pressure on the recipient's body. She said that sometimes people were quite sore after a "rolfing" session, but this meant that the internal forces and balances within the rolfee's body were out of alignment. The pain meant that the rolfer was making progress in helping the rolfee. As I asked more, the answers I got made it seem to me that "rolfing" was a pretty violent activity, but it also sounded like people kept coming back for more. They had a good business.

After awhile, I volunteered that I had just come from Washington, D.C., where they had a wonderful community rolfing program that was very informal and available to everyone; I just hadn't realized that's what it was. My patient asked me to tell her about it, so I did.

I said that, in Washington, you could just go out on the street and get rolfed anytime you wanted. You didn't even need an appointment, especially in the evenings. Somebody would come along a beat you up and take your money, but in Washington, we called this "getting mugged." In fact, this had happened to me just before I had left Washington.

Since they have an ingenious barter system in case you don't have money to pay for the service, and I didn't have any, the rolfers got my wristwatch. It was a cheap watch, so I got a good deal, but my neck hurt for a long time. In fact . . .

Well, my patient didn't like my story. She got mad. It turned out that her husband was the village rolfer where she lived. I think she misunderstood my desire to share my experiences and find common ground. Maybe she went to another doctor after that. Anyway, I didn't see her again. I was disappointed, because I was beginning to think that getting rolfed was a good thing, and I wanted to learn more about it.

MR. NICHOLLS AND THE SYMPHONY CRITICS

WHEN MR. NICHOLLS first came to Englewood in 1938, the year I was born, he rented a room at Mrs. Lorenzo's house. He had already been a school band director in another small town on the other side of Colorado for ten years.

Mrs. Lorenzo and her husband had a large truck farm a few blocks from where we lived. It was across a big field from our house and just on the other side of the irrigation ditch. By the time I got my first job at the age of ten picking strawberrys for 35 cents a flat, Mr. Nichols was no longer staying at Mrs. Lorenzo's, so it was a while before I met him.

This was my first real job. I had to show up at a certain time, I had to do what a stranger told me to do, and I got paid for doing it. It was not such hard work most of the time, but it was hot in the summer sun. Sometimes I would help Mr. Lorenzo, who spoke no English, as he harvested cabbage, cauliflower, carrots, and celery.

Mr. Lorenzo was not a talkative man, although it didn't occur to me that this was probably because we couldn't speak or understand each other's language. We got along fine as long as I figured out what he was pointing to or gesturing about and tried to do what I thought he wanted me to do. He always smelled of wine just after lunch, so I decided that Italians are people who drink wine at lunch time, and it's better to act like you don't notice. I couldn't understand why anybody would drink wine for lunch. I wasn't sure what wine was.

Mrs. Lorenzo was a small, tan, beautiful woman with warm dark eyes and grey-flecked black hair who was pleasant and cheerful and who paid me for my work. She spoke English and didn't talk funny like her husband, so I thought she was probably born in America.

It was only many years later that I learned that Mr. Nicholls had lived at Mrs. Lorenzo's house for a few years. The first time I met him, in 1954, he had already been the band director for Englewood High School for sixteen years. I didn't know that, but I knew I had better pay attention.

I played the clarinet. Mr. Nicholls had the band playing all the great classics (I didn't realize it then) such as *La Forza del Destino* by Verdi, *Der Fliedermaus* by Strauss, *Scheherezade*, the *Overture to The Barber of Seville*, *New World Symphony* by Dvorák, all the compositions of John Phillips Sousa (we were also a marching band), and popular music such as *Sleigh Ride* and the works of Gershwin. We played compositions by Bach, Handel, Mozart, Schubert, Mussorgsky, Tchaikovsky, Beethoven, Copland, Grieg, Liszt, Rossini, Vivaldi, Rachmaninoff, and Haydn, and we were expected to play them perfectly. Looking back, it was a pretty good musical education for a small-town high school.

Mr. Nicholls was a strong, confident man who appeared to know exactly what he was doing, and he got a lot of good music out of us. But one thing you couldn't do during band practice was horse around, and you dasn't horse around after band practice, either.

One time Mr. Nicholls arranged for all of us to go to hear the Denver Symphony at a rehearsal. I sat with my buddy Lynn Dhority, with whom I constantly competed for first chair in the clarinet section. Almost every other week, whichever one of us was in second chair would challenge whichever one of us was in first chair.

Something set Lynn and I off as we sat in the balcony seats listening to the Denver Symphony go through their rehearsal program. For some reason, we started shooting spitwads with a rubber band. We got the giggles. And we got thrown out.

Well, there was hell to pay with Mr. Nicholls. He brought us both into his little office that was set off to the side of the band practice room, just down the steps from the junior high cafeteria. Once inside, we stood at attention (it seemed the only thing to do), and he gave us a stern lecture on Behavior while Listening to a Rehearsal of the Denver Symphony. He told us how disappointed he was in us. "Both of you boys are from good families, and I know they teach you better manners than this," he scolded gently. Then he busted us. We would both have to go to the very end of the third clarinet section and play those boring parts. If either of us wanted to sit in first chair again, we would have to challenge everybody else in the clarinet sections, one by one. So we did.

Lynn and I both thought the whole thing was hilarious. But Mr. Nicholls treated us very seriously, and we knew he meant business. He was not a man who took this stuff lightly, but that's all he did to discipline us. Of course, Lynn and I rose up through the section within a few weeks to hold first and second chairs, and we continued to challenge each other. But we minded our manners, especially if we thought someone we knew was around. Mr. Nicholls and his wife attended the same church our families attended, and we didn't want our folks to know about the bust. I was afraid to run into him with my parents at church, but nothing ever happened.

Many years later, after Lynn and I had both graduated from college, Mr. Nicholls revealed to me that he thought shooting spitwads at the Denver Symphony was exctly the appropriate critical response, and he said he almost burst out laughing a few times, he thought it was so funny, but we never guessed. He was a good actor as well as musician, and we were skeered.

ETIR YPRINU NKRENKRE

Etir yprinu nkrenkre

—Ghanaian proverb

EFFICIENCY AND PROGRESS REPORT

Received:

DATE: 1 JUNE 1968
FROM: USPHS COMMISSIONED CORPS
      OFFICE OF OVERSEAS OPERATIONS
      SPECIAL DUTY PEACE CORPS PHYSICIANS

TO: SR SURG WARREN M HERN MD
     PEACE CORPS PHYSICIAN
     DUTY POST: SALVADOR, BAHIA, BRAZIL
     TOUR: 1 JULY 1966–30 JUNE 1968

RE: EFFICIENCY AND PROGRESS REPORT

REQUIRED AS TOUR COMPLETION DATE APPROACHES PLEASE
FORWARD POST REPORT OF EFFICIENCY AND PROGRESS TO
THIS OFFICE

Sent:

DATE: 2 JUNE 1968

FROM: SR SURG WARREN M HERN MD
      PEACE CORPS PHYSICIAN
      DUTY POST: SALVADOR, BAHIA, BRAZIL

TO: USPHS COMMISSIONED CORPS
     OFFICE OF OVERSEAS OPERATIONS
     ATTN: SPECIAL DUTY PEACE CORPS PHYSICIANS

RE: EFFICIENCY AND PROGRESS REPORT

WE'RE INEFFICIENT AS HELL AND WE'RE NOT MAKING ANY
PROGRESS STOP SORRY ABOUT THAT REPEAT SORRY ABOUT
THAT

CHICAGO 1968

In the beginning of 1968, I was serving as Peace Corps physician in Salvador, Bahia, Brazil. I was there on assignment from the U.S. Public Health Service, which had the responsibility for providing the Peace Corps volunteers with medical care. My tour of duty was to end in July.

Three years earlier, as I began my internship in Panama in 1965, Lyndon Johnson was sending many young men to Vietnam. A lot of them trained at the military installations in the Canal Zone. I took care of some of those who came into Gorgas Hospital crazy on drugs and injured in fights. They were 18-, 19-year-old athletes, in top physical form, the cream of American youth. The intern on surgery night duty rode shotgun in the ambulance, so I picked a few of them up off the pavement fatally injured in motorcycle accidents. One was thrown off the road down into the jungle. I jumped out of General Westmoreland's path as he strode across the beach at the Fort Amador's Officer's Club where he was taking a break from the war.

I didn't like the war. I thought it was wrong. The Vietnamese looked like my people in Peru, the Shipibo, as they were herded into Strategic Villages (concentration camps) and their thatch huts set on fire to flush out Viet Cong. I saw the Vietnam War as a colonial war, as a civil war, as a war that the Vietnamese were fighting to free themselves first from the Chinese, then the French, now the Americans. Later, I read *Fire in the Lake* by Frances Fitzgerald and understood this better. I had started seeing American Cold War foreign policy in a highly skeptical way years before when I had traveled in West Africa in 1961. In Nigeria I had talked to the South African survivors of the Sharpeville shooting. In Ghana, my African friends felt the U.S. State Department had conspired with Kwame Nkrumah to repress them. In Conakry, I talked with Guineans who had seen Sekou Toure's plea for help in saving his nation turned down by John Foster Dulles, only to be scorned as a communist for accepting survival help from Russia. Students in Nicaragua, who were budding Sandinistas in 1962, invited me to watch an anti-American rally, then took me to a party and told me about their American-supported dictator, Somoza. Guatemalan students told me about the American overthrow of a democratically-elected Jacobo Arbenz by the CIA. I had thought the Bay of Pigs invasion was a catastrophe for the Western hemisphere. And I knew that Ho Chi Minh was a fervent nationalist who had admired the Declaration of Independence but who was also turned down by the Americans from whom he sought help. I thought the American war in Vietnam was stupid and destructive.

184

Before the Vietnam build-up, I had decided to go into the Public Health Service in order to serve my military obligation. I wanted to work with the Native Americans in the American Southwest, in Arizona or New Mexico. Their cultures fascinated me. I also thought I wanted to do something positive instead of going to help support a killing force in Vietnam. I saw the kids I took care of at Gorgas going off to be cannon fodder in a historic military train wreck. I couldn't keep them from being maimed and killed, and I couldn't change the policy. So I tried to do something positive that mattered.

The Peace Corps volunteers who came to Gorgas from South America wanted me to come there as a Peace Corps physician. Some volunteers from northeast Brazil begged me to come there. I wanted to go back to Peru. When I was asked for my preference for assignments, I put down Peru first and Brazil second. Since I spoke Spanish, they sent me to Brazil where they speak Portuguese.

Meanwhile, my previously requested assignment to the Public Health Service Indian Hospital in Fort Defiance, Arizona, didn't pan out. My buddy at Fort Defiance, who was chief of the obstetrics and gynecology service and who had been my chief resident when I was a medical student, didn't get around to answering my letter until I had had to make a choice, so I went with the Peace Corps in Latin America. His letter caught up to me when I was leaving for language training in Portuguese.

The Peace Corps volunteers in Brazil were bright, energetic, idealistic young people who really wanted to help the Brazilians, and they did. They were nurses, teachers, mechanics, farmers, carpenters, social workers, or sometimes just kids out of college who wanted to Do Good. They were great. For awhile, the war in Vietnam seemed like a long ways away.

The Brazilians were wonderful. I loved the people, the language, the music, the food, the art, the colors, the rhythms, the legends, the folklore, the vibrancy of the place. I fell in love with an American, then she left. I fell in love with a Brazilian woman, and it was the most beautiful thing that had ever happened to me. I learned to play the guitar and started playing Brazilian music. I composed a song. I loved my work. Brazilian and American jazz musicians would come to my place after concerts at the Vila Velha and we would jam in my dining room until dawn.

In 1967, I helped my Brazilian medical colleagues get U.S. AID funds to go to an International Planned Parenthood Federation meeting in Santiago, Chile, and I went there on a busman's holiday. There were a thousand people there from all over the world, many whose names I knew from the medical literature. Some of those I met and got to know, like Rolando Armijo from Chile, Alan Guttmacher, and Christopher Tietze, were already giants in the field. Others,

such as Nafis Sadik, a Pakistani obstetrician, came to prominence later. Nafis became head of the UN Population Fund. I met people from the University of North Carolina School of Public Health who invited me to come there to study epidemiology with another hero of mine, South African physician John Cassel. So I began making plans to go there after my duty was over in Brazil in mid-1968. Cassel wrote me wonderful letters, helped me get a study grant, and became my adviser.

In late 1967, I brought my parents, who had never been out of the United States, and hardly out of Kansas or Colorado, to visit me in South America with my sisters. I used all of my savings, but we hopped around Brazil as far south as the Falls of Iguaçu and finished in the Inca ruins in Peru. When I returned to Brazil, I started hearing a lot more about the war.

My college roommate was killed as he stepped on a mine in Da Nang. He was just a year out of medical school.

 186

The Tet Offensive happened at the end of January in 1968. I listened to the BBC shortwave radio reports at night in my apartment looking out over the bay. The African sounds and rhythms of Candomblé, the Afro-Brazilian religion, floated up to me from the fishing village down by the edge of the bay. A young Brazilian man with a fantastic voice sang *Coqueiro de Itapoã* as he walked up the road from the port at midnight. The sounds of the tragedy in Vietnam came to me at the same time.

Some friends I knew from Colorado and Panama came to visit. They brought a heart-breaking letter from one of their friends, a doctor serving in Vietnam, who described the war. It was horrible.

Gene McCarthy almost won the New Hampshire primary. He was eloquent. He thought like a poet and a statesman. He made sense. He inspired me.

Bobby Kennedy announced that he would run for President.

Lyndon Johnson announced that he would not run for re-election.

Martin Luther King was assassinated.

Bobby Kennedy won the California primary and was assassinated a few minutes later.

The war kept building up, going on, getting worse. We were bombing Southeast Asia to the stone age. We were destroying the forests, the rice paddies, the villages, the people, their society, their culture. We were destroying ourselves. We were killing our best young people and destroying those who survived.

Meanwhile, the U.S.-backed military government in Brazil was coming unraveled. There were demonstrations and it started to look dangerous. I got letters from American friends saying they were worried about me. I wrote back saying that I was a lot more worried about what was happening in my own country.

When the time came, I didn't want to leave Brazil. I wanted to stay and learn Brazilian music. I loved a Brazilian woman who wanted to stay in Brazil, get married, and have babies right away (she was a little older than me), and she knew I wasn't ready for that. I didn't think I was quite ready for that just yet. She thought I would be unhappy if I stayed for her. She called it a *"desencontro"*—a "missed meeting"—too soon for me, too late for her. I didn't know what to do.

During my last week in Brazil, I had rented an apartment in Rio. One evening, we heard a man screaming and the sounds of blows. We opened the window that looked out on the courtyard of a police station. They were torturing a prisoner.

I felt very unsettled. I wanted to go to Prague to watch Dubček and the Prague Spring. I wanted to go to Nigeria; I had friends on both sides of the Biafra War. I wanted to go help Gene McCarthy get elected President. I wanted to just go lie on the beach with no plan and really relax, with no agenda, for the very first time in my life.

When the airplane stopped at Caracas, I wanted to get off and go to the island of Margarita. When the plane stopped in Miami, I wanted to get off there. When we stopped in Chicago, I wanted to get off and go to the Democratic Convention. It sounded like things were coming to a head there, the forces against the war were going to challenge the establishment, and something was going to happen. Bobby was dead; Gene was there; Hubert Humphrey, for all his idealism, had become an apologist for atrocity, and there was a chance to make the country change direction.

I stayed on the plane until we got to Denver. My folks were happy to see me, and we all went up to the mountains to camp out, catch fish, smell pine smoke from the campfire, and see the stars in the clear Colorado night. I slept in my hammock strung between two trees. My sleeping bag was covered with frost in the morning.

Somehow I was able to get the news on the car radio. I listened to the sounds of the Democratic Convention in Chicago. I felt uncomfortable not being there.

After we got back to town, my dad and I went down to a used car lot on South Broadway to find something I could drive back to school in North Carolina. We settled on a decrepit-looking Volkswagen Fastback (the name proved to be highly deceptive). Somehow I thought the car had more miles on it than the speedometer showed, but it was a good price. My dad haggled with the guy, and he knew a lot more about the mechanics of the thing than I did. While he worked out the deal, I sat in the little booth in the middle of the used car lot. The television was on the convention in Chicago. I watched in horror as the blue-helmeted Chicago police beat up the McCarthy supporters and other demonstrators with nightsticks. There was mayhem and madness. Gene McCarthy gave a speech in Lincoln Park. Mayor Daley looked like a thug.

At one point, Gene McCarthy's personal physician was being interviewed. He said that they were trying to set up first-aid stations to help the kids who were being beaten up, but they couldn't get any doctors to come help. I couldn't stand it.

As soon as I got home, I packed a suitcase, drove to the airport, and bought a ticket for Chicago. I got there in the late afternoon. As the airport bus drove us across the industrial wasteland between O'Hare and downtown, I saw a huge electric sign flashing above the dark buildings. The sign said, "Keep Our City Clean." Five seconds on, five seconds off, five seconds on, five seconds off, and so on.

We arrived at the Chicago Hilton. I looked for McCarthy's headquarters, I found the doctor I had seen on television, and I introduced myself. I was the second doctor there by fifteen minutes. The other guy was a psychiatrist and really didn't know what to do.

McCarthy's doctor put me in charge of both aid stations, but he first wanted me to go to the storefront headquarters on the street behind the Hilton and set up some first aid supplies and procedures there, so I did. The smell of tear gas was heavy everywhere. The kids in McCarthy's campaign office were scared, but they were staying. Most of them were college students. They were glad to have the help. We were comrades in arms.

There was a nurse named Diane who was gorgeous. I think she had been a Peace Corps volunteer in Africa. We liked each other. I never saw her again after that evening at the storefront.

When I went back to the Hilton, I helped McCarthy's people set up the first-aid station in one of the rooms they had set aside for it. We sat around talking about what was happening at the convention, who was getting hurt, where was Gene, what was he doing. Somebody told us at about midnight that we could crash in a room set aside for the first-aid people. About five or six of us found places to crash for the night on different beds, on the sofa, on the floor, or wherever we could find a level spot.

At three o'clock in the morning, somebody came banging on the door and hollering for us to get up and get out. We scrambled. We were sleeping in our clothes, anyway. We piled out into the corridor and somebody told us that the cops were dragging people out of bed and beating them up. I couldn't believe it. They wanted me to come right away to the elevator lobby downstairs to see the injured. There was a young man sitting on a chair, his head covered with blood, and I started checking him over. Within minutes, a bunch of people piled off the elevator, and Julian Bond, lithe and quiet, appeared while I was looking at the wounds. After awhile, Gene McCarthy, looking fresh but serious and concerned, came to see the injured student. He was furious. He asked me some questions. His voice was low, but he didn't say much as he looked at the wounds. The TV light shone on McCarthy's grey hair as he bent over the young man and said he was sorry it had happened. Then he left.

We took the battered students to the first-aid room and started rinsing the blood off around the wounds and shaving the hair from around the edges. I wanted to rinse out the lacerations immediately to reduce the risk of infection. The wounds would have to be sewn up, but we didn't have the materials for that, so the students would have to go to the hospital emergency room. Some members of Congress came in to see what was happening. David Douglas Duncan, the famous war photographer and a photojournalist hero of mine, came in to take pictures and find out about the incident. Martin Luther King's daughter showed up, and McCarthy's physician took her aside to comfort her. The police violence was upsetting to her.

Later, I wandered into a gathering and found myself next to Richard Goodwin as he discussed strategy and the events of the night with Gene McCarthy. Hubert Humphrey had won the nomination in a tumultuous convention characterized by walk-outs, walk-ins, insurrections, denunciation of police-state tactics by Abe Ribicoff with an obscene reply on TV by Mayor Daley, and a general nervous breakdown of the democratic process.

As I stood at the open door listening to a red-faced Hubert Humphrey defending his battered nomination before the Democratic National Committee, my heart sank. Humphrey was too compromised. He had let Lyndon Johnson run over him, as though anybody in Johnson's path could avoid that fate. It had a squalid, hopeless feel to it, the frantic speech to a numbed and demoralized group of Democratic leaders, and the despair of the young people outside seeped through the doors. Their despair flowed through the space. Hubert Humphrey knew it and couldn't hide it. It was in his voice.

I caught a bus to the airport and flew home. The next day, I packed my stuff in the new old car and headed east. By the time I crossed the Kansas line, I knew the car was a lemon, but it was too late to take it back to the turkey who sold it to me.

My first stop was not Chapel Hill but a small town in Pennsylvania, the home of an American woman with whom I had fallen in love in Brazil but who I could not be with while there. She wasn't home. She was in Atlanta, so I drove to Atlanta and we had lunch. I sang her a song that I had written about her. She liked the song, but things had changed. We said goodbye, then I drove that afternoon to Chapel Hill.

I got to Chapel Hill a week after classes started, found a room in Durham, and registered. One day while driving to class in Chapel Hill, I drove by a cross that had been burned on a hill by the highway the night before.

Jesse Helms raved on his television station that he owned in Raleigh. He put tobacco-stained Klansmen on the air to give their opinions about civil rights. I marched against the Vietnam war and worked briefly with Eva Clayton on a community health program. I quit smoking again and started running. I visited my mother's family, who lived mostly in a holler up by Beech Mountain.

In my first class in biostatistics, I wanted to ask a question, but I couldn't think of the English words. I was still thinking in Portuguese.

I missed Brazil and the people I knew there. I got a letter from the Brazilian woman I loved, and all I could do was to walk around and read it over and over again. She missed me, but told me I should go on with my life and she would, too. I missed her and it broke my heart. I didn't know what to do, but I thought I should stick to my plan.

Nixon won the election, and the war continued. I studied public health, sometimes with tears in my eyes.

TWO THINGS TO DO WITH LOVE

The first thing to do with love
Is to embrace it, cherish it, and share it.

The second thing,
If you cannot do the first,
Is to deny it.

You have found a third thing to do with love:
Mock it,
Suffocate it,
Strangle it and
Club it to death
Before it can be experienced and enjoyed,
Before it flourishes and multiplies,
Before it can renew itself and give life,
Before it can bother you.

That failing,
Lacerate it with the razors of bewildering rage,
Burn it with the hot poker of terror, and
Torture it
In the place where love is born
Until it is hollow with pain.

Then, maybe, it will go away.

WITH THIS RING

With this ring
I promise to give you
My constant love
The adoration I feel for you
Passionate affection
My devoted companionship
Fatherhood of our children
Partnership in our journey
My help in your becoming all you want to be
An honored place in the community
An interesting life
I am ready to give you
All my love
Not just some of it

You have taken my love
Promised me love
Not by words but by movement and being
By touching and caressing lovingly
In the night and in the light
And thrown it away
Denied our lives
Giving me just enough love
To hope
But not enough
To live

To what hidden place in your heart
Has scurried your love
Out of sight of those who would know
It is part of you?

Is your shame for loving me
Too much to bear
And is it shame for my being
Or for yours?

Did you lie
Or just deny?

Shall I try
Or die?

CERTAINTY

Who says I'm dogmatic?

I am not dogmatic.

RE: IRAQI GIRL LOSES PARENTS IN CHECKPOINT SHOOTING

(January 19 front-page photograph)

What are we doing in Iraq? The horrifying picture of the little girl, screaming in fear, splattered with the blood of her parents, who were just shot by American soldiers, tells us what we have become in Iraq: a monster of blind cruelty, an agent of destruction, and symbol of despair. That painfully eloquent photograph tells the world that what we bring is not hope and freedom but terror and pain.

The Denver Post is to be congratulated for publishing this unforgettable photograph by Chris Hondros above the fold on the front page so that the American people can see what madness we are really imposing on the people of Iraq. This chilling image overwhelms the lies told to us by George Bush and his henchmen for two years. How much more of this catastrophe, how much more torture, how many more of our troops maimed and killed, their own families at home destroyed, will it take for the citizens of this country to wake up and demand it stop?

—Warren M. Hern, M.D.
Boulder

PRESIDENT BUSH SACRIFICING LIVES TO WIN AN ELECTION

There is a truthful but tragically painful answer to Cindy Sheehan's question for President Bush: Why did my son die in Iraq? The answer: He died to keep George W. Bush in power in 2004. All other explanations or rationalizations for the Iraq war are delusional, transparently false, or have proven to be fraudulent. This one cannot be admitted publicly, especially by George W. Bush and his courtiers.

Bush has stated repeatedly that he is a "War President." He swaggers around in a flight suit after being landed on an aircraft carrier that is carefully positioned to avoid showing San Diego in the background and then declares "Mission Accomplished." He is full of machismos such as "Bring 'em on" that belie his own history and reveal his deadly adolescent fantasies.

In 1972, under Richard Nixon, we had the "Committee to Re-Elect the President." In 2003, we started The War to Re-Elect the President. It worked.

Americans don't want to believe that they are being led by an ignorant man who is so cynical, corrupt, and callous that he would start a war and sacrifice thousands of young Americans to consolidate his power, but they are. That is the unbearable answer to Cindy Sheehan's question.

—Warren M. Hern, M.D.
Boulder

THE HERN EDIBLE IUD
INSERTION TRAINING DEVICE

In 1972, when I returned to Colorado from serving most recently as an officer in a federal family planning program for the poor, I was hired as part-time medical director a family planning training program run for Region VIII of HEW by a private consulting firm. My job was to go around to all the family planning projects in the Rocky Mountain region and see what the local people needed for their programs. Also, part of my job was to teach family planning clinical and program skills to doctors, nurses, health educators, and other people running these programs. This specifically included, among other things, teaching doctors and nurses how to insert intrauterine devices (IUD's) for women who wanted them to prevent pregnancy.

There was no easy way to do this without subjecting the first patient of each doctor or nurse to the possible danger of bad technique such as perforation of the uterus. There were no teaching devices available (that I knew of) which permitted each person learning the technique to do it on an object that couldn't be hurt. So I decided to invent one.

Out in my dad's carpenter shop, I found a few pieces of scrap wood about ½ x ½ inch thick and 6 to 8 inches long. I hammered them together to make a little framework that would sit on a table. It had a couple of square ribs over the top that would support the right object. There was another frame at the leading edge where I could suspend an open vaginal speculum with a rubber band.

Then I went the grocery store and picked out a couple of nice, ripe acorn squashes. With a vegetable knife, I carved a rather authentic-looking uterine cervix in the side of one of them. Then I poked a hole in the middle to represent the external os (opening) of the cervix and made sure the small hole just the size of a cervical canal went all the way through the wall of the squash. I decided that the seeds inside would provide the proper uterine wall resistance for the insertion of the IUD by the practicing doctor or nurse.

I propped the acorn squash in my little wooden framework at the right angle, fixed the open speculum in front of the carved cervix with a couple of rubber bands, and tried it. It worked beautifully. And it worked perfectly for the doctors and nurses who tried it. They could practice all the little moves and components of the insertion such as sounding the cervix with the right pressure and depth, placement of a clamp on the cervix, and injection of anesthetic. Just learning how to put the IUD into the uterine cavity before withdrawing the covering of the IUD, and doing this smoothly, was a challenge. The practitioner had to learn how to take the IUD out of the package using sterile gloves,

199

fold down the arms of the IUD (in case of the "Copper T") and then push the device backwards down into the insertion catheter, hold it properly while also holding the tenaculum (clamp) on the woman's cervix, then insert it gently at the correct angle to just the right point into the uterus, hold the insertion catheter in place with the fourth and fifth fingers, press the plunger, and withdraw the catheter at the same time. This needed to be practiced by each doctor or nurse before subjecting their first terrified patient to this process. Fumbling and cursing does not instill confidence in the patient.

The disadvantage of my Hern Edible IUD Insertion Training Device was that you couldn't buy one from a factory: you had to make it, which meant you had to have access to a messy carpenter shop with lots of little pieces of wood lying around, some six-penny finish nails and a couple of strong rubber bands, and you had to be able to buy a good quality acorn squash. It required an excellent vegetable knife with a sharp point, a knowledge of cervical anatomy, and a sculptor's eye for the perfect cervix. Add a uterine sound and an IUD in its package, and you could start.

The singular advantage of the Hern Edible IUD Insertion Training Device was that it could solve the problem of dinner. First, after the training session, you cut the acorn squash in half on the long axis and remove the seeds along with any left over intrauterine devices that couldn't be retrieved by the trainees. Place each half of the acorn squash, cut side up, in a small cooking dish; add a half cup of water; sprinkle a little sugar, cinnamon, nutmeg, powdered cloves, and allspice on the cut surface; cover; and place in an oven at 350°F for about an hour. Serve. (Each acorn squash serves one person, unless there is something else to eat).

THIS... IS A PERSON.
NO!
IT'S *A CHICKEN!!!*

THIS...

1. Be it enacted by the people of the state of Colorado:
2. Article II of the constitution of the state of Colorado is amended BY THE ADDITION
3. OF A NEW SECTION to read:
4.
5. **Section 31. Person defined**
6.
7. AS USED IN ARTICLE II, SECTIONS 3, 6, AND 25 OF THE COLORADO
8. CONSTITUTION, THE WORDS "PERSON" AND "PERSONS" SHALL INCLUDE
9. ANY HUMAN BEING FROM THE MOMENT OF FERTILIZATION

IS A TURKEY.

On November 4, 2008, the people of Colorado will be asked to approve or disapprove the above Ballot Initiative #36 "Definition of a person." It's not on the ballot yet, but as soon as its sponsors find 76,000 certifiably stupid people in Colorado to sign their petition, it will be on the ballot, and you, the voter, will have to choose. The U.S. Constitution defines a person as existing from the moment of live birth. Initiative #36 is unconstitutional on its face. If adopted, it would mean that live birth is not a significant legal event.

This idea has many absurd and catastrophic consequences, but the principal purpose of its sponsors is to outlaw safe abortion. Read on. Here is my editorial on this matter published in *The Colorado Statesman* on July 27, 2007.

HERN: WOULD A FERTILIZED EGG NEED A PASSPORT?

When is an egg not an egg?

An egg is a person. No, an egg is a chicken. A fertilized human egg is a person. An acorn is a tree. A seed is an apple. A set of plans is a house. A blastocyst is a "pre-born baby." An

WARREN HERN
GUEST COLUMNIST

adult human being is a "pre-dead corpse." Up is down. Black is white. War is peace. Facts are not important. Belief is what matters. And people who know the truth will tell you what to believe.

Anti-abortion fanatics have been saying for decades that a human embryo — or even a fertilized human ovum — is a person. The "Human Life Amendment" was introduced in Congress in 1975 by U.S. Sen. Jesse Helms. It defined a fetus as a person. Colorado's anti-abortion fanatics now want to define a fetus as a person existing "from the moment of fertilization." Their purpose, of course, is to outlaw all abortions.

The U.S. Constitution refers to "All persons born...," not "all persons conceived..." or "all fertilized eggs...." No live birth, no person. To be sure, this is an arbitrary judgment that is defined by

our culture. In some cultures, a person does not exist until the first three or six months or first birthday has passed.

Among the Shipibo Indians of the Peruvian Amazon, with whom I have worked and studied for over 40 years, a baby is not given a name — and therefore personhood — until it is at least 3 months old. There is an important reason for this. In some Amazon villages, as many as 20-30 percent of the children die before they are a year old. A child's death hurts.

Stating that a person exists from the moment of live birth solves a practical problem. It is almost impossible to know when conception, however defined, occurs. Does conception mean the moment that the sperm penetrates the covering of the ovum, or does it mean when the fertilized ovum (zygote) divides and forms a morula (clump of 16 cells)? Does conception occur when a blastula (hollow clump of cells) forms, or does conception refer to implantation of the blastocyst into the endometrial surface of the uterine wall? What if the fertilized egg gets hung up in the Fallopian tube and forms an ectopic ("out of place") pregnancy that can easily kill the woman?

Does it matter that a woman may spontaneously abort ("miscarry") a pregnancy before she is even aware of it? Does it matter that this may happen

in at least 75 percent of all conceptions? What about a spontaneous abortion (miscarriage) that happens when the woman is aware of the pregnancy? This happens in about 10-15 percent of all known pregnancies. Is the spontaneously aborted embryo a person? What if the woman smokes or drinks or takes drugs or rides the roller-coaster or hangs out with weird people? Is she guilty of homicide if she has a miscarriage because some or all of these activities are known or thought by some to cause damage to the embryo or cause a miscarriage? Who will document this damaging behavior, and who decides what is damaging?

Does the census-taker count each known pregnancy as a person? What if there are twins or triplets? Who would know this, and how would they find out? Must each woman submit to a pregnancy test or a vaginal-probe ultrasound exam? How accurate are pregnancy tests? Which tests? There are various kinds with various levels of sensitivity. What if the positive pregnancy test is registering a hydatidiform mole (a kind of pregnancy that does not result in formation of an embryo), a choriocarcinoma (a kind of highly malignant cancer) or a chorioadenoma destruens (another kind of cancer)? Are these pregnancies counted as persons? They all resulted from fertilization of an

ovum by at least one sperm.

How will the positive pregnancy test counts affect the census, and how will this affect political representation? Are districts in which women use less birth control likely to get more representatives because there are more fertilized eggs and embryos that count as persons? How will the people living in high birth-control use (or low-fertility) districts feel about having less representation than fetuses, embryos and even hydatidiform moles? Senior citizens may not like this.

If women object to being forced to submit to regular pregnancy tests, we can just throw them in jail as they did during Romania's communist dictatorship under Nicolae Ceaucescu from 1965 to 1989. Women were required to produce children in order to have more workers and soldiers. After all, that's what women are for, right?

If a pregnant woman gets a passport, does she also get one for her 6-week embryo? How will immigration authorities know if a legally registered woman is not sneaking an unregistered and undocumented embryo into the country? The border patrol will need a lot of pregnancy tests.

Warren M. Hern, a physician, is director of the Boulder Abortion Clinic.

WHEN IS AN EGG NOT AN EGG?

By Warren M. Hern

An egg is a person. No, an egg is a chicken. A fertilized human egg is a person. An acorn is a tree. A seed is an apple. A set of plans is a house. A blastocyst is a "pre-born baby." An adult human being is a "pre-dead corpse." Up is down. Black is white. War is peace. Facts are not important. Belief is what matters. And people who know the truth will tell you what to believe.

Anti-abortion fanatics have been saying for decades that a human embryo – or even a fertilized human ovum—is a person. The "Human Life Amendment" was introduced in Congress in 1975 by Senator Jesse Helms. It defined a fetus as a person. Colorado's anti-abortion fanatics now want to define a fetus as a person existing "from the moment of fertilization." Their purpose, of course, is to outlaw all abortions.

The US Constitution refers to "All persons born . . .", not "all persons conceived . . ." or "all fertilized eggs . . ." No live birth, no person. To be sure, this is an arbitrary judgment that is defined by our culture. In some cultures, a person does not exist until the first three or six months or first birthday has passed.

Among the Shipibo Indians of the Peruvian Amazon, with whom I have worked and studied for over forty years, a baby is not given a name—and thereby personhood—until it is at least three months old. There is an important reason for this. In some Amazon villages, as many as twenty to thirty percent of the children die before they are a year old. A child's death hurts.

Stating that a person exists from the moment of live birth solves a practical problem. It is almost impossible to know when conception, however defined, occurs. Does conception mean the moment that the sperm penetrates the covering of the ovum, or does it mean when the fertilized ovum (zygote) divides and forms a morula (clump of sixteen cells)? Does conception occur when a blastula (hollow clump of cells) forms, or does conception refer to implantation of the blastocyst into the endometrial surface of the uterine wall? What if the fertilized egg gets hung up in the Fallopian tube and forms an ectopic ("out of place") pregnancy that can easily kill the woman?

Does it matter that a woman may spontaneously abort ("miscarry") a pregnancy before she is even aware of it? Does it matter that this may happen in at least seventy-five percent of all conceptions? What about a spontaneous abortion (miscarriage) that happens when the woman is aware of the pregnancy? This happens in about ten to fifteen percent of all known pregnancies. Is the spontaneously aborted embryo a person? What if the woman smokes or drinks or takes drugs or rides the roller-coaster or hangs out with weird people? Is she guilty of homicide if she has a miscarriage because some or all of these activities are known, or thought by some, to cause damage to the embryo or cause a miscarriage? Who will document this damaging behavior, and who decides what is damaging?

Does the census-taker count each known pregnancy as a person? What if there are twins or triplets? Who would know this, and how would they find out? Must each woman submit to a pregnancy test or a vaginal-probe ultrasound exam? How accurate are pregnancy tests? Which tests? There are various kinds with various levels of sensitivity. What if the positive pregnancy test is registering a hydatidiform mole (a kind of pregnancy that does not result in formation of an embryo), a choriocarcinoma (a kind of highly malignant cancer), or a chorioadenoma destruens (another kind of cancer)? Are these pregnancies counted as persons? They all resulted from fertilization of an ovum by at least one sperm.

How will the positive pregnancy test counts affect the census, and how will this affect political representation? Are districts in which women use less birth control likely to get more representatives because there are more fertilized eggs and embryos that count as persons? How will the people living in high birth-control use (or low-fertility) districts feel about having less representation than fetuses, embryos, and even hydatidiform moles? Senior citizens may not like this.

If women object to being forced to submit to regular pregnancy tests, we can just throw them in jail as they did during Romania's communist dictatorship under Nicolae Ceaucescu from 1965 to 1989. Women were required to produce children in order to have more workers and soldiers. After all, that's what women are for, right?

If a pregnant woman gets a passport, does she also get one for her six-week embryo? How will immigration authorities know if a legally registered woman is not sneaking an unregistered and undocumented embryo into the country? The border patrol will need a lot of pregnancy tests.

SEGUNDINA AND JOHN

About a week after I arrived in the village, Segundina died. Rosalina was one of her daughters. I had been called to Segundina's house on the day after I arrived because she was one of those who was very ill. Segundina, a woman of about seventy-five or eighty, could no longer walk. She was lying under a mosquito net on a straw mat on the ground. Her family had placed a lot of fine river sand all around her bed since she could not walk to the bushes to *"hacer su necesidad."* Her grandchildren brought her food and clean sand. She was in pain from her bones. Julio thought she had cancer of some kind. She also had tuberculosis. By now she had edema in her legs, probably from congestive heart failure, because it also developed in her arms within a few days. She itched all over. I thought she also might have kidney failure. Her family stayed near. There were always three or four family members waiting on the floor of the kitchen by her mosquito net. Sometimes she would sit up and eat a little. Then she couldn't sit.

She moaned with pain and moved to escape it. With the little medicine I had, there was not much I could do except to try to make her comfortable.

Finally, one morning, a wail went up from that part of the village. Segundina had died. Her daughters, female cousins, and granddaughters gathered by her corpse, now wrapped in handspun cloth, to wail. Rosalina was there with her sisters. The women covered their heads with dark shawls and sat cross-legged along the edge of the kitchen. They wailed the Shipibo death song, a minor key, ringing with sadness, and the words gave tribute to their mother, aunt, cousin, as she was to them. Segundina's grandsons made a casket from a canoe. That afternoon, they took her to the cemetery.

I could not help comparing the death of Segundina, who died with her family and friends gathered by her for the final vigil around the clock—they knew death was approaching—to the death of my father, who died several years ago in a local hospital, well attended by the Intensive Care Unit crew, but without his friends. Here was a man who had thousands of friends who would do anything for him and loved him, and who had a family who loved him, but who died virtually alone; who faced the terror of death without someone he loved close by his side all the time. We could not know that this was the time because we had pulled him back from the brink so many times; my sisters could not be there each visit to the abyss because they lived so far away, my mother was incapacitated from a serious injury, and I was attending my own patients, whom I could not leave. I could only call the hospital between each of them. He's getting air better. His oxygen saturation is up. We just moved him to ICU. He's holding his own. He's comfortable.

He opened his eyes with all his effort to look at me when I got there, but he couldn't talk with all the tubes. He nodded a little. And then he sank. The line between life and death became not a last breath but a glowing green line on a glass screen. There was no wailing, but there was no one to hear. Death came alone.

When I wheeled my mother in to see him, he was gone. The ICU people had tried and tried, but it was no use. They were removing the tubes, the artificial veins and sinews, our equivalent to the Shipibo *hanshítote wiwa!*, the "song by which we hold back death," but there was no medicine man to sing that beautiful melancholy minor chant, no silent kinsmen gathered around to sit on the old overturned canoe and share our grief, only the sound of electronic monitors humming along without a stimulus or response in the ether out there. He was gone. He was at peace. And we couldn't get him back. The end of life was bandaged in wires and curtains.

My mother pulled herself up from the wheelchair and, ever so gently touching his face, leaned over and kissed him. "Johnny," she said. After awhile, we left.

For us, there was pain without a wound.

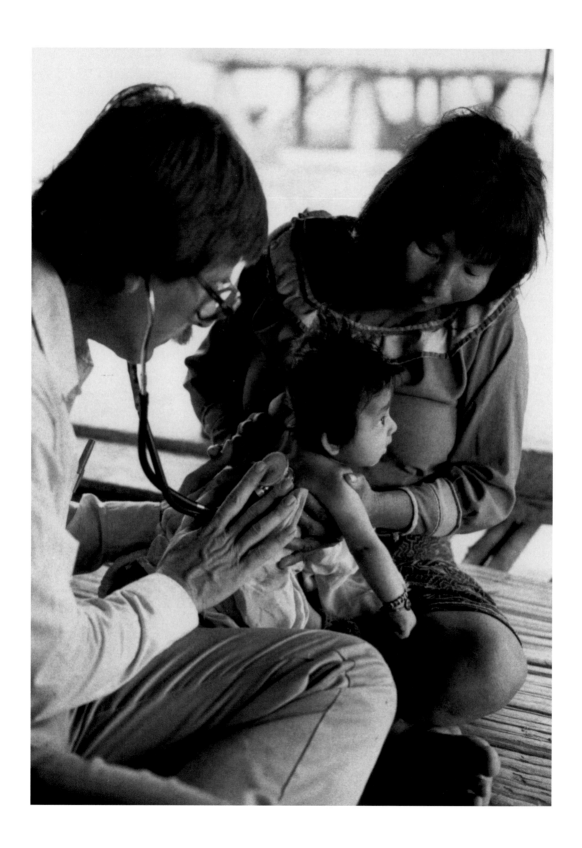

NOTES

IT MAY NOT BE CUSTOMARY to write explanatory notes about poems—after all, "A poem must not *mean*, but *be*" (Archibald MacLeish).

Just the same, I thought it might be fun or interesting as well as illuminating for the puzzled reader of these poems (or whatever they are) and stories to know what is behind some of them. For one thing, the context is significant, and while I find it challenging to understand some poems without the context, and it may be the decent thing to leave the context out, I have sympathy for the curiosity of someone who really wants to know.

"Prostate Power" was written in 1970 when I was working in Washington, D.C., and the Congressional seniority system kept some truly senile and igno-rant old men from letting the country go forward. So was "Complicity." Richard Nixon was President. I was a civil servant, not a political appointee, you understand.

The title poem, "Risus Sardonicus," was written in 1968, while I was about to end my service as a Peace Corps physician in Brazil, seven years after I had seen an Ibo baby dying of tetanus in a bush hospital in Abakaleke, Nigeria. "Risus Sardonicus" means "sardonic smile" in Latin; in this context, it is the peculiar and diagnostic facial expression shown by tetanus victims as the fatal disease is causing all the muscles—including the facial muscles—to go into permanent spasm. At the time (1961), I was in between college and medical school and traveling on the Experiment in International Living Program in Nigeria. I was in the country for about two months, living with African families and learning about all aspects of African life. Abakaleke is in the eastern region of Nigeria.

"Swamp Soldier" captures the words of a man whom I saw in the emergency room while I was doing my internship at Gorgas Hospital in the Canal Zone in 1965–66. The man was, I believe, a veteran of the military who had dropped out and was living out in the jungle.

"Brazilian Girls," the form of which is inspired partly by my hilarious hero Ogden Nash, was written in the pre-feminist era, obviously. I include it for reasons of historical perspective.

"Misery" was written in Washington, D.C., in 1970 at the beginning of the women's liberation movement.

"Huiniti" is a Shipibo saying. The Shipibo people of the Peruvian Amazon, with whom I have lived and worked since 1964, are one of the great and creative tribes of people in that part of the world. They are described a little in "Up the Ucayali" and in "Segundina and John." They are my friends and family, and I am of them. I am an adopted member of the tribe. My Shipibo name is *"Caibima,"* which means "the traveler who comes from afar but who always returns." I do scientific research among them, but I also attend the sick, help deliver their babies, mourn the loss of my friends, grieve with my friends their losses, marvel at the beauty and dark moods of the Amazon floodplain and jungle, joke with them, play games with them, and listen to their healing songs in the night. I lie on the dry season beach in the Amazon night looking at the stars with my Shipibo buddies as they tell me what the constellations mean to them and listen to the cayman and big fish hunt the smaller fish in the river a few meters away. They tell me many things that matter.

One is this proverb. *"Huiniti"* is my name for it. That is the infinitive form of the verb "to cry." Shipibo is an agglutinative language, different from Western languages, and combines words to make a new meaning. *"Huinitajahuequi"* combines two words *"huinita,"* which roughly means "something sad enough to make you cry," and *"jahuequi,"* or "thing." *"Moa"* means either "a long time ago," or "already past," sort of the equivalent of *"ya"* in Spanish. *"Shinanti"* is the infinitive form of the verb "to think," and *"ma"* is negative, something like "non-" in English as in "nonsense." The whole phrase, or actually, sentence, is pronounced thus: *"WEENEETAH HOWEEKEE MOWAH SHEENANTEEMAH."*

Try saying it and listen to the poetry and rhythm of this phrase. The accent is on the first syllable of the first three words and on the second syllable of the fourth word. *"Shinantima"* actually ends with a glottal stop, as in the non-sound at the end of the English words "hit," "bat," and "stop." There is no break between any of the words while pronouncing the Shipibo. Aside from its sheer poetic and linguistic beauty, the concept expressed in the proverb tells us important things about the Shipibo culture and even something of Shipibo survival strategies. The Shipibo live in a harsh and unforgiving environment that has its wonders and beauty, but it is a world in which death and loss are a part of everyday life.

The approximate English translation of the proverb would be, "We no longer think about the things that are so sad they make us want to cry." The translation, of course, cannot convey the depth of feeling, the beauty, and the economy of expression one experiences in the Shipibo original, particularly in the context of the culture and the moment in which it is spoken. It is a great privilege to hear this language and know these people. I thank them for an indispensable part of my life.

The short poem "SUAVE®" requires a little background explanation to be appreciated. In 1983, I went to the Peruvian Amazon, where I had traveled and worked many times since 1964, to conduct my research for my Ph.D. in epidemiology (I was studying the health effects of cultural change among the Shipibo Indians). Because I was working in remote Shipibo villages that required long trips by dugout canoe for weeks and months at a time, I had to take all the supplies with me that we needed. A necessary item was a bale or two of toilet paper, and the most ecologically correct toilet paper was SUAVE®, which was supposed to have the added advantage, according to its name, of being "suave" (soft). This toilet paper—supposedly biodegradeable—was so ecologically correct that it came complete with its own wood splinters. Its consistency was somewhere between crepe paper and emory board. I concluded after several months in the field that SUAVE® was probably not degradeable by any known chemical process. I discovered wilted banana leaves and managed to escape my research experience without a perineal skin graft.

"Great Bringer of Death to Paradise" is about what is now the Holy Cross Wilderness in Colorado. When I was very young, long before it was officially declared a federal Wilderness, I went to Homestake Lake many times with my father. We would drive up the old Gold Park Road, go to a campground near the falling-down old cabins left by the gold rush in the last century, pitch a tent, then hike up the valley to fish in the beaver dams above Homestake Lake. The first time we went, around 1950, I was about twelve years old. This is where my dad taught me to fish.

In 1965, the cities of Aurora and Colorado Springs built a dam across the Homestake Valley and flooded the area that we had visited including the marshes and beaver dams above the old natural Homestake Lake that had been left by the glaciers. The poem resulted from a solo trek I made about 1990 to see the upper Homestake Valley where I used to fish with my father. Because of the dam and the reservoir covering the old meadows, natural lake, and upstream inlet, getting there now requires going up a side canyon, over a high pass, and dropping down through a very isolated area of benches and small lakes to the old headwaters instead of walking up Homestake Valley, which has been turned into a bomb crater.

In 1982, I started the Holy Cross Wilderness Defense Fund with some backpacker friends to stop construction of the Homestake II Project that would have destroyed the rest of the wilderness. We have stopped it, for now.

I am not optimistic for the rest of the planet.

My comments as a scientist about this general subject of the effect of human species on the planetary ecosystem can be found in two issues of *Population and*

Environment [1990:12(1),9;1999:21(1),59] and in *BioScience* [1993:43(11),768]. On-line versions of these articles may be found at www.drhern.com/articles.asp?ID=42.

"Reading Copy" is a speech I delivered on the front steps of the Boulder City Hall on February 12, 1995, during a candelight vigil for those who had been killed by violent anti-abortion fanatics. Six weeks before, John Salvi had walked into two Boston clinics and shot five persons, of whom two died. Three doctors had been assassinated in 1993 and 1994, a Canadian doctor was critically wounded in an assassination attempt, a doctor friend of mine was shot in both arms in an assassination attempt, a doctor's bodyguard had been killed, and several other people critically injured. On January 22, 1995, three weeks before this speech was given, a group calling itself the American Coalition of Life *[sic]* Activists held a press conference and announced a hit list of the first thirteen abortion doctors they wanted eliminated. I was on the list. From that point, I was placed under the 24-hour armed guard of U.S. federal marshals except during the time I was giving this speech. Authorities said they could not protect me if I chose to speak in public. For this speech, I was brought to the back door of the City Hall in a secure vehicle with two private armed guards. I was met at the back entrance by the police SWAT team and brought into the City Hall, which was evacuated and secured, and I was held inside until it was my time to speak. My friends, standing in the subfreezing weather and holding candles, waved at me through the front window of the City Hall. The crowd of about 200 was patrolled by uniformed officers, plainclothes detectives, and and numerous federal law officers who could not be there officially. A man who had been stalking me and said that he wanted to kill me because I do abortions had just been released from jail. The police expected a sniper attack from him or someone else. I was wearing a bullet-proof vest. A beloved, grandmotherly former schoolteacher and state legislator, a dear friend, was almost shot by alarmed police when she ran across the stage at me to give me a warm hug. It was a bitterly cold evening, and the hug was good. I was escorted back inside and taken away as soon as I gave my speech.

Since then, Eric Rudolph was sent to prison for killing an off-duty policeman and maiming nurse Emily Lyons at an abortion clinic in Alabama in January 1998, as well as other crimes, including the Atlanta Olympic Park bombing. Another physician who performs abortions, Dr. Bernard Slepian, was assassinated by James Copp in 1998. Authorities suspect that he was the person who shot and almost killed a physician who does abortions in Vancouver a few years earlier.

"Paraweasel" was written while I was sitting in a federal courtroom in Portland, Oregon as a plaintiff in civil trial of anti-abortion fanatics who had issued a hit list of the first thirteen doctors they wanted eliminated. The list, issued at a press conference in January 1995 included my name. Three of my colleagues who provide abortion services and who were targets of this madness were in the courtoom with me at the time (January through February 1999). We were sitting next to a large group of defendants who wanted us dead. One of their paralegals, a dark, short, hair-slicked-back man in a black suit, looked sinister to us as we watched him scurry around the courtroom doing the dirty work of our adversaries. We began calling him the "paraweasel." Toward the end of the trial, he came up behind me surreptitiously and hit me on the back with a sub-poena so as to "serve" me and tie me up in court for an extended period during appeals or such maneuvers. The judge quashed the subpoena and forbade such tactics in the courtroom.

I believe that "If You're a Good American, Stand Up!" is the first thing I ever wrote that appeared in print. It was the result of a field trip report for a political science class at the University of Colorado at Boulder.

"Un viaggio interessante con una conclusione sorprendente e piacevole" was written in re-sponse to a request by an Italian tutor that I write a paragraph about my trip to Italy the previous year (1995). Although I had passed through Italy in 1961 on my way to West Africa (my face pressed against the bus window as we went by the Colisseum in the evening on the way to the airport), the 1995 visit was my first time back since then. I had been invited by an Italian anthropology professor to speak in Florence at an international conference on evolution and demography.

I took the occasion to intensify my study of Italian, spending a week at the conference and two weeks traveling around the country. I pretended to be a Brazilian who didn't speak English, but some doorman at a jazz concert in Matera (southern Italy) guessed that I was a "fiorentino" from my Florentine accent. I could barely stand to get back on the plane, which I almost missed because the traffic in Rome.

My Italian friends wanted me to come back to Rome, where I could do abortions to make a living. "But what about the Pope?," I asked. *"Il Papa è per gli turisti,"* they would say ("The Pope is for the tourists!").

Finding that speaking Italian is right up there in the range of sensuous experiences with making love and skiing on fresh powder, I decided to go back to Florence the next year to study the language for a whole week (all the time I could take from my medical practice at that point). In preparation, I decided to hire an Italian tutor. At a local Italian restaurant, there was a charming young graduate student from Venice who tutored Italian. Being Venetian, she was unfortunately very businesslike, but she was a good teacher. As an exercise, she asked me to write a paragraph in Italian about my visit to her country the previous year. *"Un viaggio interessante . . ."* is the result of that exercise. You should have seen her face when I recounted my visit with the Pope.

"Hay cerveza?" recalls a consistently serious but unknowingly hilarious response of a Peruvian shopkeeper, José, who kept a small but generally bare *tienda* (store) on the corner and just down the lane from the hospital where I worked in 1964. My buddy, Frank Billman, and I would drift down to Jose's plain, unpainted little shop on a hot afternoon to see if we could buy a cold beer. But often, there was no beer at all, much less cold beer, in the humble establishment whose interior was lighted only by the reflected glare of the dusty plaza across the street.

Rather than admit the scarcity, however, José, with natural dignity, genuine remorse, and unassailable logic, would tell us, "Yes [there is beer], but we don't have any." It was a perfectly honorable and diplomatic solution to an awkward problem. It was a solution that applied broadly in all local village businesses that encountered shortages of beans, canned tuna, gasoline, motor oil, writing paper, and toilet paper. It was, after all, the last town in the jungle at the end of a long, muddy (and sometimes impassable) road from Lima.

"Mr. Brooks" captures the words and a little of the magnificent spirit of a man I knew in Tennessee. In 1971, when I was working as a public health physician in the Office of Economic Opportunity Family Planning Program in Washington, D.C., I was called to see about funding a program in voluntary sterilization for the poor people of Anderson County, Tennessee. The people running the program were conscientious and dedicated, and they found that their constituents, the coal miners and tradesmen of the Appalachian hollers, were desperate to limit their fertility, especially after they and their wives had eight or ten children. The wives were worn out from childbearing and begged for help. The male outreach worker of the program was a man named Bob Brooks, who worked (as I remember) as a maintenance supervisor at the Oak Ridge atomic energy plant. Bob was a simple man with a limited education, but he was extremely intelligent, dedicated, and highly sensitive to the needs of his neighbors in the remote hollers of Anderson County. I went out with him to visit these people and I will never forget the experience. He was wonderful, and the stories told by the people were touching. (My article about this appeared in *The New Republic* magazine in March 1971 under the title, "Biological Tyranny.") The poem is simply one of the things that Bob told me about how he worked

215

with the people to understand them, gain their confidence, and help them with their needs. I regard Bob as a great man who made a tremendously important contribution to the lives and welfare of his fellow citizens.

"Etir yprinu nkrenkre" means "My first allegiance is to my own mind." It is from the Twi language spoken in Ghana. In 1958, when I was an undergraduate at the University of Colorado and living in Baker Hall, a student dormitory, I was reading the paper in the student lounge one day and found myself sitting next to an African man who appeared to be a visitor. I struck up a conversation with him. He was a Ghanaian journalist named Henry Ofori who was visiting the United States on a State Department-sponsored tour. Since I was keenly interested in Africa and knew that Ghana had just gained its independence, I wanted to learn as much as possible from him. Henry was very friendly and spoke to me at length about the African independence movement, the cultural and economic changes in West Africa, his family, his work as a journalist, and his interest in learning about America. He told me that he was the editor of *Drum Magazine*, one of the principal magazines in his country, and that he wrote a column under the pen name of "Carl Mutt." As we talked longer, Henry told me that he would like to get a bottle of Johnny Walker Black Label Scotch. It was illegal to bring liquor into the dorm, and I had never bought liquor in Boulder, but I said sure, let's go find out where to buy some. We got in my car, drove around Boulder, which was a pretty small town then, and found a liquor store that was open. When we got back, I checked to see if any campus police were about, and we took the Scotch to Henry's room. He opened the bottle and then conducted a ceremony whereby he poured a little of the very expensive liquor on the floor while chanting something in his language. He told me he was making an offering to the gods, which is traditional when one is about take a drink with a friend. Then he poured a little Scotch in two glasses. We drank Scotch (I never finished mine—I didn't like it) and continued talking into the night. As we were about to end our conversation, he said he would teach me an important proverb which was his favorite—*"Etir yprinu nkrenkre."*

Henry and I stayed in touch after he returned to Ghana. He would always put this proverb at the end of each letter after his signature. I started looking for ways to visit Africa since I had been inspired to go into medicine by the example of Albert Schweitzer. I somehow learned of the Experiment in International Living Program out of Putney, Vermont. They had a program that took young people to various foreign countries and arranged for "homestays" so that one would find out what family life was like in the country. Nigeria was a "pioneer" country because the living conditions were sometimes difficult, certainly by comparison with conditions in Europe. But the cost was $1,400, and I didn't have that kind of money. The Experiment had a "Community Ambassador Program" through which various organizations would contribute money to send a young person to a country in the program, then return and give reports about the experience to the organizations. Englewood, Colorado, did not have a "Community Ambassador Program," so I started one. I thought it would be a good idea, anyway, because the local newspaper editor was against the United Nations and against having anything to do with other countries. I think he was also against languages other than English. Other people would just have to give up their languages and learn to speak English.

Many organizations in Englewood responded to my presentations and requests, and pretty soon I had more than enough. I even got a scholarship from an organization that helped the Experiment In International Living. The result was that in the summer of 1961 I went to Nigeria for two months with this program. This was when I went to the hospital in Abakaleke in the eastern region of Nigeria and saw the baby dying of tetanus ("Risus Sardonicus").

Since I had a little money for independent travel, I parted with my group at Kano, Nigeria, and flew back to Lagos. They went on home through Paris. I met the Prime Minster of Nigeria, Alhaji Sir Abubakar Tafawa Balewa, with whom I had corresponded before going to Nigeria. He was an extremely gracious and pleasant man who was assassinated in a coup d'etat a few years later.

My first stop after leaving Lagos was Accra, Ghana, where I was met at the airport by Henry and his wife, Rosemund. I stayed with them and their children for a week. I had a wonderful time. Rosemund, a nurse, was also an excellent cook. She made Ghanaian peanut soup that was one of the best things I ever tasted.

By this time, Henry was no longer the editor of *Drum Magazine*. During his trip to the U.S., which had been arranged by the Ghanaian government headed by Kwame Nkrumah, Henry received a call from Accra during which he was told that, because of his magazine commentary that had been critical of Nkrumah (who called himself *"Osagyefo"*—"The Savior"), Henry would agree to resign his editorship and become a civil servant in the Ministry of Information creating propaganda for Nkrumah after his return to Accra—or he would not see his family again.

At the end of all the letters I ever received from Henry over the years, he always included the proverb, *"Etir yprinu nkrenkre"* after his signature.

Later, after Nkrumah, Henry became the editor of the *Ghanaian Times*, the government newspaper.

When I tried to make Ghanaian peanut soup back in Colorado, it set up like concrete. It's a good thing that nobody in our family ate much of it.

PHOTO NOTES

Title page and cover: Shipibo hand-woven, hand-painted cloth.

Frontispiece: Little Falls, East Cross Creek, Holy Cross Wilderness. (1986)

Page 3: Woman with smallpox, Hospital Amazonico "Albert Schweitzer." This was the last smallpox epidemic in the Western hemisphere. (1964)

Page 4: The Shipibo *muraia* ("seer") Benito, looking at my microbiology book. (1964)

Page 5: Luis "Lucho" Ramirez Cairuna, whose house was at the port to Paococha and whose son died just before we arrived at dawn to bring the smallpox vaccine in 1964. (1984)

Page 6: Augusto Flores, a schoolboy who came walking through the vaccination line at the village of Roaboya. He had a malignant chondrosarcoma. His leg was removed at the hip socket in Lima in time to save his life. (1964)

Page 9: Heliodoro "Helio" Maynas Maldonado. We were close friends from the time we met in 1964 until his death in 1996. He was a champion athlete, community leader, loving father and husband, philosopher, diplomat, expert hunter, fisherman, and navigator of the Ucayali River; companion, mechanic, raconteur, and a very nice man. (1984)

Page 25: Lasthenia Ramirez Cairuna "Inimue" ("sweet-smelling herb" in Shipibo). Mother of my friend, German Cairuna Ramirez, youngest wife of Leoncio "Suisane." She was as serene and kind as she looks in this picture. (1984)

Page 26: Leoncio Cairuna Ramirez "Suisane." Father of German Cairuna Ramirez, husband of Lasthenia Ramirez and Zoila Ramirez. He was as funny and mischievous as he looks in this picture. (1984)

Page 27: Zoila Ramirez Cairuna, sister of Lasthenia, oldest wife of Suisane with a newborn great-great grandchild. (1989)

Page 28: Jabiru storks on the Ucalayi River, looking for small fish during the *mijano* (dry season fish spawning migration). (1984)

Page 29: Zoila Ramirez Cairuna. (1989)

Page 30: Maria, a great-great grandmother, whose daughter Isabel has been one of my best friends since 1964. I stayed with Isabel, her husband Carlos, and their children in 1969 and 1974 when I was doing research in Paococha. Maria's husband, Pastor Ochavano, was my principal informant for anthropological research in 1964. (1984)

Page 31: Eva Inuma. I have known her and her family since 1964. One day in 1984, her husband Oligario came to me to tell me that Eva had abdominal pain. I went to examine her. She had an "acute abdomen" (rebound tenderness in the abdomen when the hand pressing down is suddenly removed), which indicates peritonitis, usually fatal in this setting. The story was that Eva had a little bump at her umbilicus that bothered her a little bit when she was carrying or chopping wood. She was seen by a local *sanitario*, a kind of medical corpsman, who looked at it and decided that Eva had an abscess. So he stuck a needle in it to drain the abscess. Then she really got sick. She probably had a loop of bowel in a small umbilical hernia, and this inadequately trained and overzealous medic stuck a needle into her bowel, thereby releasing the intestinal contents into the peritoneum and starting a potentially fatal infection. I immediately started her on heavy antibiotics, of which I had few, kept her on bed rest, no food except liquids, and she survived. Amazing. Most people would just die. Eva is tough. (1984)

Page 32: Woman carrying water from the river at dawn. Typical handmade Shipibo pot. (1984)

Page 33: Rosalia sitting on a mat and weaving with a back-strap loom in the yard by her house. She is the woman who gave me the necklace as I stepped out of the canoe and into the mud at the "port" of Pucallpa in 1974. (1984)

Page 34: A handpainted *jonichomo* Shipibo pot. *Joni* means "person" in Shipibo and *chomo* means "pot." This photograph was taken at the cooperative craft store "Maroti Shobo" set up by missionaries and Dutch development workers to help the Shipibo sell their museum-quality handcrafts, especially pottery. It was successful until the terrorist movement, Sendero Luminoso ("Shining Path") shut down Peru's tourist trade in the 1980s and 1990s. (1984)

Pages 35 and 36: Jacoba Urquia, also a master potter and weaver, sister of Florencia. She is painting designs on her *jonichomo* pot with a strand of her hair. (1984)

Page 37: Jacoba Urquia, my dear friend from 1964. (1984)

Page 38: My dear friend Selmira Obillus sculpting a pot. In 1964, she had a terrible and dangerous dental abscess. I gave her antibiotics and she survived. Since then, she greets me warmly and makes up songs about me. She is a master at the Shipibo crafts. Photographs of her are included in an exhibit in the Hall of South American Peoples at the American Museum of Natural History in New York. (1989)

Page 39: Florencia Urquia, one of the great artists among the Shipibo and a friend since 1964. Florencia's daughter is married to Helio. Her sister is

Jacoba Urquia. At the time of this picture, the village was flooded, but she continued her work in her kitchen. (1984)

Page 40: Spinning cotton in the late afternoon. Archeologist Don Lathrop stated that the only cotton in the world that has the same genetic pattern as the cotton used by the Shipibo is found in Southeast Asia. (1984)

Page 41: Leonora, weaving a bolt of cloth. (1984)

Page 42: Kids playing with bubbles. (1984)

Page 43: Spinning cotton in the afternoon. (1984)

Page 47: Mr. Foo in the medical ward of Gorgas Hospital, Canal Zone. (1965)

Page 52: Triple waterfall, East Cross Creek, Holy Cross Wilderness. (1986)

Page 54: Homestake Lake, a natural glacier-formed lake, as it looked in 1955 before the Homestake Dam was built over it, destroying the valley. (1955)

Page 56: Cross Creek at the base of Long Meadow just above the confluence with East Cross Creek. (1986)

Page 58: Long Meadow (9,800-foot elevation), Holy Cross Wilderness. This meadow would be destroyed by the proposed Homestake II Water Diversion Project planned by cities of Aurora and Colorado Springs. (1986)

Page 62: My father, John W. Hern, Jr. (1912–90), working on the roof of my house in the mountains. He was a master craftsman. (1973)

Page 66: Pink Fairy Slippers (*Calypso bulbosa*) an orchid found on the banks of small streams flowing into Cross Creek. This is one of the rare plants that would be destroyed by the Homestake II water diversion project. (1982)

Page 67: Holy Cross Mountain and Mount of the Holy Cross at dawn; from Notch Mountain. I got up before dawn and took my view camera, 35mm camera, and tripod out to the edge of the top of Notch Mountain to get this among other pictures. I had a head lamp so I could see the rocks pretty well, I thought. When it got light, I could see that I was only about a meter from the edge of a cliff that dropped about 500 feet. The Holy Cross Wilderness is named for the snow-filled crevasses that make the cross formation seen in this picture. Its National Monument status was repealed in the 1950s so that the Homestake I water diversion project could be built. (1989)

Page 68: Cross-country skiing in the Holy Cross Wilderness. (1985)

Page 70: Cross Creek, winter. This photograph appeared in the *1988 Sierra Club Engagement Calendar*. (1985)

Page 71: One-sided Penstemon (*Penstemon unilateralis*), Gilpin County, Colorado. (1980)

Page 84: Silvia, victim of a terrible skin disorder, village of Nueve de octubre (1984)

Pages 86, 87: Silvia, village of Nueve de octubre. (1984)

Page 88: Alfie and his mother, Nueve de octubre. (1984)

Page 89: A young American nurse, Linda, reassures a Shipibo girl suffering from intestinal parasites. (1984)

Page 92: The village of Nuevo Eden at the foot of the Cordillera Azul, the western boundary of the Amazon and the easterly range of mountains leading to the Andes. This is the youngest mountain range in South America—about 14 million years old. Nuevo Eden is the last Shipibo village on the upper Pisqui River, a tributary of the Ucayali, which becomes the Amazon at the town of Iquitos in Peru. (1990)

Page 94: Taking bananas and other food to children studying at the high school down the river at Charasmanan, Nuevo Eden. (1990)

Page 121: Dr. Michael Diana looking over a patient before beginning surgery at the Hospital Amazonico "Albert Schweitzer." (1964)

Page 123: Rosa Torres, our scrub nurse, me, and Dr. Diana at the operating table, Hospital Amazonico "Albert Schweitzer." (1964)

Page 125: Rosa Rojas at the hearth in her kitchen by the lake, Paococha, in the village of the same name. Rosa was the woman we operated on for cervical cancer a few weeks before this picture was taken. She died that year. (1964)

Page 126: Pablo Macedo, my dear friend, dying of tuberculosis in 1974. He was one of my best friends in Paococha. He was the husband of Rosa Rojas. (1974)

Page 127: A young American nurse, Linda, gives medicine to a Shipibo child. (1984)

Page 128: Me with some large trout I caught (with steel leaders) while fishing a previously unexplored stream in the headwaters of the Pisqui. We were trying to get to a legendary salt deposit ("Tashi manan"—"Hill of Salt") that had been used for centuries by the Shipibo who traded the salt with other tribes for things they needed. We were trying to get there, but the river had washed out their traditional route, so I suggested we try another approach. The Shipibo didn't know about this stream until I showed them where it was with a map and satellite photographs. We used my compass and transit readings to get there. (They thought I was crazy, but what the hell.) Since the stream we found didn't have a name (very unusual for any geographic landmark, meaning they really didn't know about it), they named it after me. So the stream is now called "Huian Caibima" (Caibima Creek). This picture was taken on our second trip up into the newly-discovered stream. We explored up several kilometers before we were threatened with a flash flood. We barely escaped with our lives. (1992)

Page 130: My friend Victorino Rojas, a master hunter of *paiche (Aripaima gigas)*, the largest freshwater fish in the world, shown with a small specimen. The Shipibo men stand in a tiny 2–2.5-meter dugout canoe and harpoon these animals with a weapon that weighs about 10 kilos. (1984)

Page 134: Julio Linares, the village *sanitario* (health corpsman) administering two intravenous lines that I started on a woman in Nuevo Eden who was dying from cholera. She lived. Julio is smart, dedicated, and conscientious. (1991)

Page 136: Octavio Linares, the patriarch of Nuevo Eden. It was easy to imagine Octavio as Chairman of the Joint Chiefs of Staff or President of the United States. (1991)

Page 148: Edna Hern, my mother, just before her 90th birthday. (2007)

Page 151: Englewood High School athlete Kay MacFarland at the 1955 State Track Meet. This picture won second prize in the 1956 Eastman Kodak High School Snapshot Contest.

Page 154: South American Jaguar *(Panthera onça)*. Manu National Park, Peru. (1985). This appeared on the covers of *1987 Sierra Club Wildlife Calendar* and the book *Celebration of Life* (1997).

Page 156: Roseate Spoonbill *(Ajaia ajaja)* in flight, Mermentau River, Louisiana. This photograph appeared in the *1989 Sierra Club Engagement Calendar*. (1979)

Page 158: Roseate Spoonbill chicks in nest, Mermentau River, Louisiana. 4 x 5 view camera. (1979)

Page 160: Juvenile Great Egret stretching at dawn, Mermentau River, Louisiana. (1979)

Page 161: Roseate Spoonbill family feeding young at nest, Mermentau River, Louisiana. (1979)

Page 162: Great Egrets at dusk, Mermentau River, Louisiana. (1979)

Page 164: Upper Kintla Lake, Glacier National Park, Montana, at sunset. (1978)

Page 166: Tarn on Boulder Pass, Glacier National Park, Montana, at dawn. (1978)

Page 168: Hole-in-the-Wall Creek, Hole-in-the-Wall Basin, Glacier National Park, Montana. (1978)

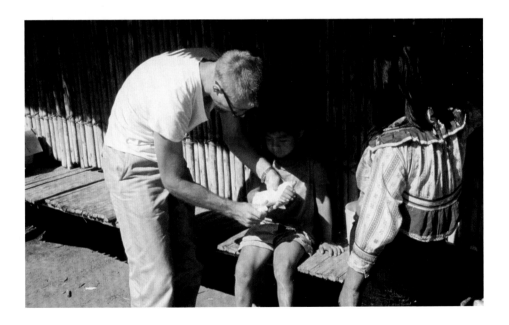

ABOUT THE AUTHOR

WARREN MARTIN HERN is a physician and epidemiologist who practices medicine in Boulder, Colorado, and teaches from time to time at the University of Colorado.